FOR THE LOVE OF THE LORD

FOR THE LOVE OF THE LORD

Letting Love Transform You into the Person God Wants You to Be

Nancy Ferguson

FOR THE LOVE OF THE LORD
Letting Love Transform You into the Person God Wants You to Be

Copyright May 2010 by Nancy Ferguson
ISBN 978-0-89112-679-9
LCCN 2010017060

Printed in the United States of America

Unless otherwise noted, Scripture quotations are taken from the HOLY BIBLE, NEW INTERNATIONAL VERSION®. Copyright © 1973, 1978, 1984 Biblica®. Used by permission of Zondervan. All rights reserved. Scripture quotations noted ERV are taken from the HOLY BIBLE: EASY-TO-READ VERSION © 2001 by World Bible Translation Center, Inc. and used by permission. Scripture quotations noted KJV are taken from the King James Version of the Bible. Scripture quotations noted NLT are taken from the Holy Bible, New Living Translation, copyright 1996, 2004. Used by permission of Tyndale House Publishers, Inc., Wheaton, Illinois 60189. All rights reserved. Scripture quotations noted NRSV are taken from the New Revised Standard Version Bible, copyright 1989, Division of Christian Education of the National Council of the Churches of Christ in the United States of America. Used by permission. All rights reserved. Scripture quotations noted RSV are taken from the Revised Standard Version of the Bible, copyright 1952 [2nd edition, 1971] by the Division of Christian Education of the National Council of the Churches of Christ in the United States of America. Used by permission. All rights reserved.

LIBRARY OF CONGRESS CATALOGING-IN-PUBLICATION DATA
Ferguson, Nancy, 1934-
 For the love of the Lord : letting love transform you into the person God wants you to be / Nancy Ferguson.
    p. cm.
 Includes bibliographical references and index.
 ISBN 978-0-89112-679-9
 1. Love--Biblical teaching. 2. Love--Religious aspects--Christianity. I. Title.
 BS680.L64F47 2010
 241'.677--dc22

2010017060

Cover design by Nicole Wilson

Leafwood Heritage is an imprint of
Abilene Christian University Press
1626 Campus Court
Abilene, Texas 79601

1-877-816-4455
www.leafwoodpublishers.com

10 11 12 13 14 15 / 6 5 4 3 2 1

*To my children and grandchildren
as they continue to live for the love of the Lord.*

Table of Contents

Preface 11

Chapter One: What Is Love, Anyway? 13

Chapter Two: Live a Life of Love 23

Chapter Three: God's Love Transforms 33

Chapter Four: God's Love Protects 45

Chapter Five: Love and Marriage 59

Chapter Six: Love Makes Marriage More Meaningful 71

Chapter Seven: Love Your Children 83

Chapter Eight: Make Your Children Feel Loved 101

Chapter Nine: Love One Another 115

Chapter Ten: Love, the Most Excellent Way 127

Chapter Eleven: Love Serves 149

Chapter Twelve: A Loving Servant 159

Chapter Thirteen: Love Is the Answer 171

Endnotes 183

Scripture Index 187

Acknowledgments

I am indebted to my loving husband for the valuable help and encouragement that he always gives me.

Preface

It has been said that love is the most powerful force in the universe. Because God is love, this statement is obviously true. But what is love? How does it make us act? How does it change us? These and other questions deserve to be studied carefully. The purpose of this book is to do just that.

The Bible has much to say about love, but we all too often let our preconceived notions get in the way of understanding God's message. This book is not an exhaustive study of love, but it is intended to help you better understand what the Bible teaches about love.

My prayer is that as you read this book, you will learn more of God's love and be drawn closer to the source of the unlimited love lavished upon us daily. It is not enough merely to learn about love; it is essential to let that love transform you into the person God wants you to be.

This book is written from the perspective of one who firmly believes that the Bible is the inspired word of God and that it is as relevant for us today as it was when it was written.

CHAPTER ONE

WHAT IS LOVE, ANYWAY?

"God is love."
—1 John 4:8,16

We use the word "love" in many different ways. For instance:
"I love to go camping."
"I love my children."
"I love to sleep late on a cloudy morning."
"I love broccoli."
"I love my husband."
"I love to go walking in the rain."
"I'd love for you to have dinner with us Friday!"
"I love your new dress."
"I love God."
"I love people, but I can't stand So-and So!"

So, what do we mean when we use the word "love"? Is it "like"? "adore"? "care for"? "enjoy"? "have passionate feelings for"? Or is it something else?

What does the Bible mean by "love"? By looking more closely at the way the word is used in the Bible, we can gain a better understanding of the concept of love.

The title of this book deliberately has a double meaning, for it refers both to the love that God has for us and to the love that we have for God. God doesn't just tell us he loves us; he shows us. God's love for us explains why Christ came to earth: "For God so loved the world that he gave his one and only Son, that whoever believes in him shall not perish but have eternal life" (John 3:16). Also, 1 John 3:16 describes this same love: "This is how we know what love is: Jesus Christ laid down his life for us."

Likewise, our love for God is not expressed merely by our saying, "I love you, Lord," but mainly by our actions in obedience to him: "This is love for God: to obey his commands" (1 John 5:3). Our lives should be lived for the love of the Lord.

The ultimate definition of love is given in 1 John 4:8, 16: "God is love." Thus, if we want to know what God means by love, we need to know God himself.

The Greeks Had Words for It

The Greeks had at least four words that are translated into the one English word, "love." Because they had several words, they could be more precise in their discussions. Looking at the meaning of these words and seeing the differences among them will help us to be more precise in our understanding of what the Bible says about love. In the pages that follow, transliterations of Greek words appear in italics.

1. *phileo, philia*

The main idea of *phileo* (verb form; noun form, *philia*) is affection or fondness. The *New International Dictionary of New Testament Theology* describes it this way:

> [P]*hileo* is the most general word for love or regard with affection.... [It] mainly denotes the attraction of people to one another who are close together both inside and outside the family; it includes concern, care and hospitality, also love for things in the sense of being fond of....
> The main emphasis of *phileo* is on love for people who are closely connected, either by blood or by faith.[1]

This defines the love we have for those with whom we share our faith in God and our love for him. We are fond of each other in a special way because of our relationship with God and with each other. Friendship is also included in this word.

We are familiar with "phil-" in the context of several common English words, including Philadelphia ("love of brothers" or "brotherly love"), philosophy ("love of wisdom"), philanthropy ("love of mankind"), and philharmonic ("love of harmony"). These words indicate a special interest in the topics described, just as we have special feelings for those with whom we have much in common.

2. *stergo/storgeo, storge*

Stergo mainly refers to love within one's family. Returning to the *New International Dictionary*, we read:

> The less frequent word *stergo* means to love, feel affection, especially of the mutual love of parents and children. It can also be used of the love of a people for their ruler, . . . and even of dogs for their master. . . . It . . . does not occur at all in the NT, apart from the compounds *astorgos* (Rom. 1:31; 2 Tim. 3:3) and *philostorgos* (Rom. 12:10).[2]

The negative compound, *astorgos*, is translated in various versions of the New Testament as "heartless," "without love," "inhuman," "unloving," or "without natural affection." And *philostorgos* means "love of brothers in the family," "mutual affection," or "heartfelt love."

3. *eros, erao*

The main idea of *eros* is sexual desire:

> The vb. *erao* and the noun *eros* . . . denote the love between man and woman which embraces longing, craving and desire. . . . Sensual ecstasy leaves moderation and proportion far behind. . . . [The Greeks] knew the irresistible power of Eros—the god of love bore the same name—which forgot all reason, will and discretion on the way to ecstasy.[3]

Eros, a word not found in the New Testament, also describes the so-called love that selfishly desires to have, to grasp, or to take possession: that is, lust.

These three words deal with what we might call "reciprocal" love, the kind that works both ways. There is mutual affection among members of a family. We feel kindly toward someone who is kind to us. As a man and a woman are falling in love, their love is strengthened as they realize that they each return shared feelings of affection.

The Greeks had a fourth word, *agape*, that refers to a different kind of love. We might call this one-way love. A person does not need reciprocation from another in order to exercise *agape* love. It is the way God loves us. His love for us does not depend on our response—he still loves us even when we do not return his love.

4. *agape, agapao*

The main idea of *agape* is active concern for others. *Agape* (and its verb form *agapao*) in the New Testament is used in the sense of God's love—God's love for humans, humans' love for God, or the love for others that is based on God's love. "In the NT ... *agapao* and the noun *agape* have taken on a particular significance in that they are used to speak of the love of God or the way of life based on it."[4]

God can command this love because it refers to the way we act more than the way we feel. It is action more than emotion. It is love that we can decide to practice toward others no matter how we feel about them. It is caring, giving, thoughtful love. It is not selfish or demanding. It is active goodwill.

Agape puts the other person first. It never injures the object of love, for "Love does no harm to its neighbor" (Rom. 13:10). This is the love that God commanded us to have for our enemies (Luke 6:27). We may not like our enemies, but loving and liking are two different things. Remember—the love that God commands is how we act toward others, not necessarily how we feel about them. However, as we act in a loving way, feelings of affection often will follow. The school teacher who has difficulty with an unlovable student but who prays fervently about that student and treats the student lovingly will often develop strong feelings of affection for the unruly child.

Actions can be commanded, but it is futile to command feelings. For example, have you ever tried to command a child to *like* Brussels sprouts? You cannot force anyone to like anything. However, that child may decide to taste the Brussels sprouts in spite of not liking them. In the same way, God does not command us to like a certain person, but he wants us to decide to act in a loving manner toward that person, even if the person is an enemy. As a child continues to taste the Brussels sprouts over time, he or she may learn to like them. In the same way, if we continue to act as we should toward someone we do not like, we may eventually like that person.

So, to review, this definition gives us three aspects of *agape* love to consider:

1. God's love for us
2. Our love for God
3. Our love for each other based on God's love

In chapters nine and ten, we will consider more fully our love for each other, but we need to look at the other two first. It is because God loves us that we even know what love is. It is because God loves us that we want to love him in return. And it is because God loves us that we love one another (1 John 4:10–11).

God's Love for Us

In the Old Testament, God declared his love for his people in many passages of Scripture, such as this verse from Jeremiah:

> The Lord appeared to us in the past, saying:
> "I have loved you with an everlasting love;
>   I have drawn you with loving-kindness." (Jer. 31:3)

God's love for us never ends. Psalm 136 assures us in every verse that "His love endures forever." Each verse of the psalm also tells something he has done to show his love for his people: he has done great wonders;

he created the heavens; he made the sun, moon, and stars; he gives food to all creatures, and more.

> God promised us tender loving care, as in Isaiah:
> > He tends his flock like a shepherd:
> > He gathers the lambs in his arms
> > > and carries them close to his heart;
> > > > he gently leads those that have young. (40:11)
>
> and
> > As a mother comforts her child,
> > > so will I comfort you. (66:13)

It is comforting to know that God delights in his people and rejoices over us:

> The Lord your God is with you,
> > he is mighty to save.
> He will take great delight in you,
> > he will quiet you with his love,
> > he will rejoice over you with singing. (Zeph. 3:17)

Not only does God delight in his people, but he considers them his "treasured possession":

> Then those who feared the Lord talked with each other, and the Lord listened and heard. A scroll of remembrance was written in his presence concerning those who feared the Lord and honored his name.
>
> "They will be mine," says the Lord Almighty, "in the day when I make up my treasured possession. I will spare them, just as in compassion a man spares his son who serves him. And you will again see the distinction between the righteous and the wicked, between those who serve God and those who do not." (Mal. 3:16–18)

There are many more verses in the Old Testament that tell of God's great love for us, but these are enough to make the point convincingly.

As we turn to the New Testament, we find that God's love for us is almost always described by the word *agape*. It is the love that puts the loved one's interests first. It is not selfish. It does not arrogantly demand its own way. It is neither harsh nor grasping. It does what is best for the other person. It is the love that we learn about by the way God treats us.

The most important thing to remember is that God himself is *agape* love (1 John 4:16). Everything to be said about love hinges upon that important fact. Love is at the heart of Jesus's teaching: it is the very nature of God. When we love, we somehow share in God's nature. The more fully we experience love, the more wonderful we find it to be. If we as Christians follow the example of Jesus, we will love. If we claim to be children of God and yet are unloving, we lie (1 John 4:19–21).

Because God is love and the kind of love being discussed is the love that God has for us, it will be helpful to look at the ways God shows that love to us.

God Showed His Love through Jesus

The most important way that God has shown his love for us is through Jesus: "This is how God showed his love among us: He sent his one and only Son into the world that we might live through him" (1 John 4:9).

How he could love us enough to make such a great sacrifice for us is almost impossible for our frail human minds to grasp, but he did. Romans 5:8 assures us of this fact: "But God demonstrates his own love for us in this: While we were still sinners, Christ died for us." And John 13:1–2 also testifies that Jesus showed his love for us through his willing sacrifice on the cross: "It was just before the Passover Feast. Jesus knew that the time had come for him to leave this world and go to the Father. Having loved his own who were in the world, he now showed them the full extent of his love" (John 13:1–2). Jesus then washed the feet of his disciples, thus giving them an example of humble, loving service. But the "full extent of his love" is shown in something even more significant. John spends the rest of his book, chapters 13–21, telling what Jesus did to show his love for us. John 15:13 is an important part of that story: "Greater love has no one than this, that he lay down his life for his friends."

In showing us that greatest love, Jesus suffered and died on the cross, taking all our sins onto his sinless self. Sometimes we hear sermons describing the physical pain that Jesus endured for us. But even more agonizing to him was the fact that he took on himself all the sins of all humanity. That sinless one, who had never done anything wrong, who had never sinned in any way, came to know the horrible depths of sin: "God made him who had no sin to be sin for us, so that in him we might become the righteousness of God" (2 Cor. 5:21). This spiritual burden of sin was much worse than any physical suffering could ever be. Many others went through the pain of crucifixion, but only Christ suffered the agony of taking our sins upon himself. Only Christ was raised from the dead, never to die again. It is only because of his great sacrifice of love that we have the opportunity to become righteous in God's eyes.[5]

As he took our sins upon himself, he felt separated from God. He cried out "My God, my God, why have you forsaken me?" (Mark 15:34). He was quoting the first verse of Psalm 22, and when you read that Psalm, you will see that it ends in triumph:

> For he has not despised or disdained
> the suffering of the afflicted one. (Ps. 22:24)

God did not turn away from Jesus at that time. He was still there, still loving his son, but something was blocking the flow of that love. And that something was our sins. Because of all of the sins of all the world, Jesus could not feel the warmth and comfort of his Father's love. We might compare it to a cold, cloudy day. The clouds obscure the rays of the sun, and we cannot feel the sun's warmth nor see its brightness. As the cold, cloudless days continue, we may even feel that the sun has forsaken us. However, above the clouds, the sun is still there, still shining in all its glory, brightness, and warmth. In the same way, God's love will never fail, no matter what happens. Although it appeared that God had forsaken his beloved son, he had not—he still loved Jesus. The Bible assures us of that fact in Romans 8:38–39: "For I am convinced that neither death nor life, neither angels nor demons, neither the present nor the future, nor any powers, neither height nor depth, nor anything else in all creation, will be able to separate us from the love of God that is in Christ Jesus our Lord." If nothing can separate *us* from God's love, then surely nothing could separate the son of God from his Father's love, not even our sins.

My prayer for you is the same as Paul's for the Ephesian Christians: "I pray that you, being rooted and established in love, may have power, together with all the saints, to grasp how wide and long and high and deep is the love of Christ, and to know this love that surpasses knowledge" (Eph. 3:17b–19a).

―――――――― For Further Thought ――――――――

1. What is your definition of "love"?

2. How does the difference between loving and liking affect what you do?

3. How do the different definitions of the Greek words for "love" help you to understand what the Bible means by "love"?

4. What are some specific ways that God has shown his love to you?

5. What are ways that you can show your love for God? Think especially of ways not mentioned in this chapter.

6. How can you live a life of love?

CHAPTER TWO

LIVE A LIFE OF LOVE

"Do everything in love."
—1 Corinthians 16:14

"Jesus loves me" may be one of the first concepts we teach our children, but it is one of the most profound concepts that we can learn as adults. It is also one of the most difficult to understand fully. In the awe-inspiring verses in Ephesians 3:17–19, Paul prays that, even though we are established in love, we may be able to understand, to comprehend, to grasp the magnitude of the love that Christ has for us: the love that is beyond knowledge.

John says Jesus showed us the "full extent of his love" (John 13:1) by dying for each one of us because of his great love. With the limitations of our human minds, how can we grasp this incomprehensible concept? Fortunately, John helps us begin to understand: "This is how we know what love is: Jesus Christ laid down his life for us. And we ought to lay down our lives for our brothers" (1 John 3:16). Someday we will see him face to face, and then we will understand more fully the love that caused Jesus to be willing to sacrifice himself for us.

In the ancient pagan world, mankind made sacrifices to the gods to appease them, to pacify them, to make them friendly toward humans. It was a way of manipulating the gods to do what man wanted done:

> The dominant sentiment in the sacrifice was that "I give in order that you may give to me." ... Socrates says, "Sacrificing is making gifts to the gods and praying is asking from them," and

concludes ... that "holiness would be an art of barter between gods and men." The sacrifice was an exchange. The more abundant and better the offering, the more acceptable it would be.[1]

The pagan sacrifice was intended to bring the god into line with the desires of the one offering the sacrifice, and the better the sacrifice, the more the worshiper would expect to be rewarded.

However, an entirely different situation exists with the one and only Almighty God. He turned the sacrifice upside down! God, not man, is the one who offered the sacrifice to bring mankind into harmony with God, not the other way around: "He [Jesus Christ] is the atoning sacrifice for our sins, and not only for ours but also for the sins of the whole world" (1 John 2:2). He loved us enough to provide the way for us to be united with him.

Love has been described as a golden chain that binds us together. Sometimes that chain is broken because of the weakness of human beings. But God's love for us is stronger than any chain. It is so strong that it can never be broken—there are no weak links in the chain of his love for us (Rom. 8:38–39). In other words, absolutely nothing can keep God from loving us. What a wonderful, comforting concept that is!

God Shows His Love for Us Today

We know that long ago God showed his love for us by sending Jesus to die for us, but sometimes we may wonder, "How does God continue to show us his love today?" There are many ways, and perhaps the few that we mention here will help you to think of other ways that God has shown his love in your life.

We Are God's Children

"How great is the love the Father has lavished on us, that we should be called children of God! And that is what we are!" (1 John 3:1). Good parents love their children; and God is certainly a good parent (Matt. 7:9–11). He loves us and cares for us in many ways that we do not even acknowledge. God provides us with air to breathe, he makes the crops grow so we can eat, he provides us with beautiful sunsets and lovely flowers to show us what beauty is, he gives us the inner strength to overcome our problems, and he provides protection from the evil that is all around us. We could go on and on. When Thanksgiving Day approaches, many people will stop and think briefly about the blessings God has given us. But these blessings are not limited to the end of November. He blesses us and cares for us day-by-day all year long and then year after year for all of our lives. Therefore we should be grateful daily for the love that he has for us.

We Are God's Temple

God shows his love for us by giving us his Holy Spirit to dwell within us: "Do you not know that your body is a temple of the Holy Spirit, who is in you, whom you have received from God? You are not your own; you were bought at a price. Therefore honor God with your body" (1 Cor. 6:19–20).

Today, we sometimes think of a temple as a place where pagans came together to worship their idols. In New Testament times, however, the temple was considered to be the home or dwelling place of the god, not a place of assembly. There were many pagan temples in the ancient city of Corinth, so Paul knew that when he told the Corinthian Christians *they* were the temple of God, they would recognize he was saying that God would make his home, his dwelling place, within each person. That is what happens when we are baptized and are given the gift of the Holy Spirit to dwell within us.

We Can Be Confident That God Will Help Us When We Need Him

"Let us then approach the throne of grace with confidence, so that we may receive mercy and find grace to help us in our time of need" (Heb. 4:16). God does not leave us all alone to confront the problems of our lives. He is ready to help us, to extend his grace to us. This does not mean that as Christians we will never have any problems. Rather it means that God will guide us and help us to have the inner strength to face our problems and overcome them. Our prayers will be answered in the way that only God knows is best.

We Have the Hope of Salvation

Ephesians 6:10–18 describes God's armor, which he allows us to wear, and calls one of the elements of his armor the "helmet of salvation." A parallel passage in 1 Thessalonians 5:8 refers to putting on the "hope of salvation as a helmet." Romans 5:1–5 also speaks of this hope:

> Therefore, since we have been justified through faith, we have peace with God through our Lord Jesus Christ, through whom we have gained access by faith into this grace in which we now stand. And we rejoice in the hope of the glory of God. Not only so, but we also rejoice in our sufferings, because we know that suffering produces perseverance; perseverance, character; and character, hope. And hope does not disappoint us, because God has poured out his love into our hearts by the Holy Spirit, whom he has given us.

It is because of God's great love for us that we can hope to share in his glory. What a blessing it is that he continues to pour out his love on us!

As we rejoice in this hope of heaven, consider this little story that came to me by e-mail. I have no idea who wrote it.

Duct Tape Or A Nail?

A man dies and goes to heaven. St. Peter meets him at the Pearly Gates and says, "Here's how it works. You need 100 points to make it into heaven. You tell me all the good things you've done, and I give you a certain number of points for each item, depending on how good it was. When you reach 100 points, you get in."

"Okay," the man says, "I was married to the same woman for 50 years and never cheated on her, even in my heart."

"That's wonderful," says St. Peter, "that's worth two points!"

"Two points?!" he says. "Well, I attended church all my life and supported its ministry with my tithe and service."

"Terrific!" says St. Peter, "That's certainly worth a point."

"One point!?!! I started a soup kitchen in my city and worked in a shelter for homeless veterans."

"Fantastic, that's good for two more points," he says.

"Two points!?!!" Exasperated, the man cries. "At this rate the only way I'll get into heaven is by the grace of God!"

"Bingo! 100 points! Come on in!"

We often try to fix problems with WD-40 and duct tape. God did it with a nail.

AMEN

Yes, God shows his love for us by giving us the hope of salvation through his grace.

We Are Blessed by the Beauty That God Has Created

We can praise God for beautiful sunsets, roses with their delicate petals, a yellow field of daffodils in the spring, the pristine white of new-fallen snow, and many, many other wondrous beauties. God's loving care is evident in all the world of nature around us. When God created everything, he saw that it was good. And all of nature continues to be good.

SHOWING OUR LOVE TO GOD

There are many other ways that God continues to shower his love upon us every day. We need to open the eyes of our hearts and be aware of his love and mercy to us. As we see God showing his love for us, we need to find ways to show our love to God.

The first and greatest commandment is to love God with our entire being (Matt. 22:37–38). Every thought, every emotion, every desire, and every ability must be surrendered to the creator and sustainer of the universe.

Love God by Obeying Him

First and foremost, we show our love for God by our obedience to him. As 1 John 5:3 says, "This is love for God: to obey his commands. And his commands are not burdensome." And John 14:15, 21, and 23 all state very plainly that if we love God, we will obey him. That is how God wants us to show our love for him. If we say that we love God, but do not obey his every command, then we are lying—we do not really love him (1 John 2:3-4).

Consider a young man who frequently, and sometimes loudly, declares to his girlfriend and others his deep love for her. However, he seldom calls her, rarely spends time with her, and almost never does for her anything that she likes for him to do. The girlfriend would be correct in deciding that his declarations of love for her were meaningless. If he really did love her, he would spend time with her and do nice things for her. He would pay attention to see what she liked, and then he would show his love by doing what pleased her.

In the same way, we show our love for God by paying attention to his word, studying it to learn what he wants us to do, and then doing it. If we love him, we will obey him. We need to read the Bible daily to be sure we know what God wants us to do. Remember, we must obey God, not what someone else says that God wants us to do. We need to be like the Bereans, who searched the Scriptures daily to see if what they were being told agreed with God's word (Acts 17:11).

Love One Another

We are commanded to love God and to love our fellow human beings, and we cannot do one without the other. This is one of the important things that God wants us to do: "Dear friends, let us love one another, for love comes from God" (1 John 4:7). Loving fellow Christians is an identifying characteristic of those who are followers of Jesus: "A new command I give you: Love one another. As I have loved you, so you must love one another. By this all men will know that you are my disciples, if you love one another" (John 13:34–35).

The command to love one another is one that we cannot ignore. We will consider more fully in chapters nine and ten this love for fellow

Christians. For now we want to emphasize that this is a command of God that we must obey, no matter how we feel about others.

We might say, "I really don't like So-and-So very much, so why should I have to love him?" First John 4:19 answers that for us: "We love because he [God] first loved us." We were not really very lovable when Christ died for us, were we? We were not very likable, either. But God still acted in loving ways toward us. By the same token, we can act in loving ways to those whom we consider to be unlovable. We do this because God loved us first and showed us the way. He did not just tell us to love, he showed us both *what* love is and *how* to love. The passage in 1 John continues: "If anyone says, 'I love God,' yet hates his brother, he is a liar. For anyone who does not love his brother, whom he has seen, cannot love God, whom he has not seen. And he has given us this command: Whoever loves God must also love his brother" (1 John 4:20–21).

Take Care of the Less Fortunate

We read in 1 John 3:17–18: "If anyone has material possessions and sees his brother in need but has no pity on him, how can the love of God be in him? Dear children, let us not love with words or tongue but with actions and in truth." Jesus taught an important lesson for us in Matthew 25:31–46 when he said, "Whatever you did for one of the least of these brothers of mine, you did for me" (v. 40). Our benevolent acts may be done for the less fortunate, but in effect they are done for Christ himself. When we realize the truth of these words, it will be easier to love those who are, by our definition, unlovable.

Years ago, I heard a lesson from a preacher who was working with drug addicts and others with moral problems. He said that he had to concentrate on the face of the person, ignoring the unruly hair and dirty clothes, so that he could make himself think about Jesus and the fact that Jesus loves that person as much as he loves the preacher himself or anyone else. Only then could he bring himself to want to help that person.

Serve One Another In Love

We may find it difficult to love someone who is unlovable, but Paul gives us a hint of how to proceed in Galatians 5:13–15: "You, my brothers, were called to be free. But do not use your freedom to indulge the sinful nature; rather, serve one another in love. The entire law is summed up in a single command: 'Love your neighbor as yourself.' If you keep on biting and devouring each other, watch out or you will be destroyed by each other."

Jesus came to earth to serve others. Think of what he taught when he washed the feet of the disciples. Washing the feet of guests was considered to be the task of the lowliest of all the servants in the household, yet the lord and master of the universe knelt down before his disciples, and humbly and lovingly performed this act of kindness. The Lord wants us to serve others just as humbly. No task is beneath us if it needs to be done to serve someone else and to show love to someone else.

If we spend our time in loving service to one another, we will find that we are obeying what Paul says in Ephesians 5:2: "Live a life of love."

Biblical Joy

Love is surrendering to the will of the heavenly father, whether it is what we want or not. Love is saying with Jesus in the garden, "Not as I will, but as you will" (Matt. 26:39). Jesus did not want to die on the cross, but he surrendered to the will of his father in heaven because of both love and joy.

It is difficult for us to imagine that any joy could be associated with the death of Jesus on the cross, but that is what the writer of Hebrews tells us: "Let us fix our eyes on Jesus, the author and perfecter of our faith, who for the joy set before him endured the cross, scorning its shame, and sat down at the right hand of the throne of God" (Heb. 12:2).

Jesus could feel joy because he loved us and knew that what he was doing was for our good. This is not the kind of joy that is bouncing, giddy, and laughing. Rather it is that deep-down feeling of accomplishment, of knowing that what has been done was the right action, and of knowing the satisfaction of a job well done. Jesus endured the agony of the cross because he loved us and he knew that without his blood being shed there would be no hope of our salvation. Thus he could feel joy for what he had accomplished on our behalf.

If Jesus could find joy submitting to the will of his father, then we too find joy when we submit to God's will. It is when we rejoice in the Lord that we find the peace that is beyond understanding (Phil. 4:4–7). When we submit to the will of God, the Spirit dwells within us and we receive the gifts of the Spirit described in Galatians 5:22–23. The surrender may seem painful at the time, yet it is the avenue to the ultimate joy that is so desirable.

Conclusion

The whole of our lives should be spent imitating God, who is love, and acting in loving ways toward everyone: When the apostle John was young, he was known as a "Son of Thunder" (Mark 3:17). Yet, in his old age he was known as the Apostle of Love.[2] John spent his life maturing in the loving ways God wanted of him. He did this by imitating God. We, too, should mature in the love of the Lord as we grow older. We do that by living a life of love.

It is my prayer that each one of us may spend our lives doing what Paul says in Ephesians 5:1–2: "Be imitators of God, therefore, as dearly loved children and live a life of love, just as Christ loved us and gave himself up for us as a fragrant offering and sacrifice to God."

FOR FURTHER THOUGHT

1. How would you define biblical joy? How can you have it in your life, even when things are going wrong?

2. What does it mean for you to be able to "approach the throne of grace with confidence" (Heb. 4:16)?

3. How would you describe to someone else (perhaps your children, your grandchildren, or a new Christian) the meaning of the verse, "God is love" (1 John 4:8, 16)?

4. How does being the temple, the dwelling place of God, affect the way you treat your body and the way you live?

5. Think of a time when you have acted in a loving way toward someone you did not like. What happened as a result?

CHAPTER THREE

GOD'S LOVE TRANSFORMS

"Because of his great love for us, God . . . made us alive . . . even when we were dead in transgressions."
—EPHESIANS 2:4–5

When we look around us, we see much evil in the world. We see it on TV, in the movies, in the newspapers and magazines, even in the lives of people we know. Consider how many marriages are breaking up, how many lies are being told, how many lives are being hurt by the actions of Satan in our world today. Sometimes it is enough to make us give up and say, "What can we do? It's just too much for us. Satan has too strong a hold on this world. There's nothing we can do to protect ourselves from all this evil!"

However, God's love for us is so all-encompassing that he wants to protect us from evil. We need his protection. We cannot survive without it. We cannot protect ourselves alone. It is a marvelous blessing that God daily offers us his protection from all the evil in the world. Even though sometimes we may not recognize his efforts, we are assured that he is always with us:

> So do not fear, for I am with you;
>   do not be dismayed, for I am your God.
> I will strengthen you and help you;
>   I will uphold you with my righteous right hand. (Isa. 41:10)

Psalm 139 also assures us that God is with us everywhere. He knows everything about us, even our thoughts. He is always there to guide us and to help us. He lavishes his love on us in many ways, and one way is that his love protects us. One way that he protects us is by allowing his love to transform us from being lost in sin to being righteous in his sight (see 2 Cor. 5:21 and Rom. 4:8, 6:4).

The first chapter of this book listed a few of the ways in which God shows his love for us. Chapters three and four will concentrate on the way in which he demonstrates his love by protecting us from the wiles of Satan. He does this for us because of his unlimited love and mercy. God had the power to create everything in the whole universe (Gen. 1); he had the power to raise Jesus from the dead (Eph. 1:19–20); he has the power to defeat Satan and all his servants (Rev. 12:9–10); and thus he has ample power to protect us. Not only does he have the power, but we have the assurance that he will act on our behalf: "The Lord will rescue me from every evil attack" (2 Tim. 4:18; see also Ps. 121:7–8; 2 Pet. 2:9).

My prayer is that as you read this chapter, you will be convinced of the depth of the love that God has for you. I hope you will be filled with awe as you think about his mighty power, which he makes available to you. Because he is all-powerful, he is *able* to give you the protection that you need. Because he is all-loving, he *wants* to give you the protection you need. God is the almighty ruler of the heavens and the earth, and thus Satan trembles and cannot stand before him.

God's Protection

We sometimes may wonder, "How does God protect us? What does he do?" Ephesians 6:10–18 describes part of how God protects us from Satan. This is a very important and very powerful scriptural passage that was written to the members of the Lord's church in Ephesus. It is a glorious ending for a glorious book. It is just as true for us today as it was for those in the first century:

> Finally, be strong in the Lord and in his mighty power. Put on the full armor of God so that you can take your stand against the devil's

schemes. For our struggle is not against flesh and blood, but against the rulers, against the authorities, against the powers of this dark world and against the spiritual forces of evil in the heavenly realms. Therefore put on the full armor of God, so that when the day of evil comes, you may be able to stand your ground, and after you have done everything, to stand. Stand firm then, with the belt of truth buckled around your waist, with the breastplate of righteousness in place, and with your feet fitted with the readiness that comes from the gospel of peace. In addition to all this, take up the shield of faith, with which you can extinguish all the flaming arrows of the evil one. Take the helmet of salvation and the sword of the Spirit, which is the word of God. And pray in the Spirit on all occasions with all kinds of prayers and requests. With this in mind, be alert and always keep on praying for all the saints. (Eph. 6:10–18)

To show how God protects us, Paul used as an illustration the defensive armor of a soldier. Every part of this armor was important because attacks on the soldier could come from any direction. We must withstand the attacks of Satan from all directions, therefore we need all the different parts of God's armor to protect us completely and leave no vulnerable areas. But since these verses about the armor of God come near the end of the book of Ephesians, it will be helpful to look at the earlier part of the book before we reach that passage.

God's Power
In writing to the Christians at Ephesus, Paul refers to God's care and the spiritual aspects of life in this world: "Praise be to the God and Father of our Lord Jesus Christ, who has blessed us in the heavenly realms with every spiritual blessing in Christ" (Eph. 1:3 RSV). God is ruler not only of the earth but also of the heavenly or spiritual realms; as Lord of all, he alone has the power to give us all of his spiritual blessings, which help to protect us. These blessings come only to those who are in Christ. The riches of God's grace had been lavished on the Ephesian Christians (Eph. 1:6–8), even as they are on Christians today. We can see this in Ephesians 1 and 6, which make good "bookends." The book both begins and ends

with an emphasis on the mighty power of God and on God's glorious grace and strength:

> I pray also that the eyes of your heart may be enlightened in order that you may know the hope to which he has called you, the riches of his glorious inheritance in the saints, and his incomparably great power for us who believe. That power is like the working of his mighty strength, which he exerted in Christ when he raised him from the dead and seated him at his right hand in the heavenly realms, far above all rule and authority, power and dominion, and every title that can be given, not only in the present age but also in the one to come. (Eph. 1:18–21)

Our human minds cannot fathom the infinite power of God. Yet because of his great love for us, God makes his vast power available to us through faith in him. It is mind-boggling to realize that such power really can be ours. What a blessing! God's infinite power is the only thing in the universe that is strong enough to protect us from Satan. It is because of God's tender love for us that he makes this protecting power available to us. Let us constantly praise him for his love and power!

God's Love and Mercy Transform Us

Although the Ephesians were sinful when they were following the evil ruler of God's rebel subjects (Eph. 2:1–2), God's love and grace transformed them from being dead in sin to being alive in Christ (Eph. 2:5). They could not have done it themselves (Eph. 2:8–9). That same love and grace is poured out on us today, thus enabling us also to be transformed.

Paul refers to the changes that occurred in the lives of the Ephesians when they were converted to the Lord:

> As for you, you were dead in your transgressions and sins, in which you used to live when you followed the ways of this world and of the ruler of the kingdom of the air, the spirit who is now at work in those who are disobedient. All of us also lived among them at one time, gratifying the cravings of our sinful nature and following its desires and thoughts. Like the rest, we were by nature objects of wrath. But because of his great love for us, God,

who is rich in mercy, made us alive with Christ even when we were dead in transgressions—it is by grace you have been saved. And God raised us up with Christ and seated us with him in the heavenly realms in Christ Jesus, in order that in the coming ages he might show the incomparable riches of his grace, expressed in his kindness to us in Christ Jesus. (Eph. 2:1–7)

What a contrast! From being "objects of wrath" to being seated with Christ "in the heavenly realms"! What a blessing that the transforming power of God is greater than the power of Satan. What a blessing that God has mercy on us because of his great love for us. His grace in caring for us is more than we can comprehend, but we can be thankful for it.

Gentiles previously had been separated from Christ and were without God (Eph. 2:11–12). That is a terrible state in which to be. But that is not the end of the story. They had been brought near to God by the blood of Christ (Eph. 2:13). By his death, Jesus broke down the barrier that separated the Jews and Gentiles (Eph. 2:14–18). Now Gentiles could become Christians and thus members of God's household—that is, children of God (Eph. 2:19). As his children, they came under his protection. And as his children, the Gentiles became heirs along with the Jews (Eph. 3:6).

When one has lived a sinful life (as those Gentiles had done) and turns to God, Satan greatly increases his efforts of temptation to win back that person (Matt. 12:43–45). That is when we need the loving protection of God's armor more than ever. Fortunately for us God has promised that we will not have more temptations than we can handle: "No temptation has seized you except what is common to man. And God is faithful; he will not let you be tempted beyond what you can bear. But when you are tempted, he will also provide a way out so that you can stand up under it" (1 Cor. 10:13).

Prayer is an important part of that way out of temptation. Prayer is how we plug into the power of God. Gentiles (and that includes me, as well as most of you who are reading this) as well as Jews may now approach God in prayer through Christ with freedom and confidence (Eph. 3:12).

Paul's beautiful prayer is for all of us, that we may know the love and power of Christ as he works within us (Eph. 3:14–21). God's great love and tremendous power protect us from Satan.

God's Plans

God has plans for us. He gives purpose to our lives: "For we are God's workmanship, created in Christ Jesus to do good works, which God prepared in advance for us to do" (Eph. 2:10). We have been created to work for the good of others; that is our purpose in life. We show our love for God and for others by the good things we do. It is because we are constantly surrounded by God's loving protection that we have the freedom and ability to live the life of good deeds.

God gives beautiful assurance to us: "Consequently, you are no longer foreigners and aliens, but fellow citizens with God's people and members of God's household" (Eph. 2:19). Members of God's own household! That is awesome! The world around us is not really our homeland, because we are citizens of God's kingdom. We have God's power and authority to help us, because we are part of his family. He is the father of his family, and as a good father, he does everything he can to protect his precious children. But we are human children, and as such we sometimes act foolishly and then we need to be rescued from our own sins. Our heavenly father stands ready to forgive us, and to deliver us from the evil we bring on ourselves. As part of his family, he has allowed us to approach his throne of grace with confidence to ask for forgiveness. Our trust in him leads us to this confidence.

God's Wisdom

God's wisdom is shown in his plans for his church from the beginning. The church is important to God and thus should be to us, also: "His intent was that now, through the church, the manifold wisdom of God should be made known to the rulers and authorities in the heavenly realms, according to his eternal purpose which he accomplished in Christ Jesus our Lord.

In him and through faith in him we may approach God with freedom and confidence" (Eph. 3:10-12).

Satan and all his cohorts, as well as the angels in heaven, know the infinite wisdom of God. This wisdom was revealed through the church—not through the individual people who make up the church, but through God's divine plan. It was his plan from the beginning to bring us collectively to him in Christ and through his church. The church was not an afterthought, as some people try to claim. God's plans were made long before he accomplished them in Christ Jesus. The church is so important that Jesus came to earth not only to die for us, but also to establish his church. It is through the church that we must continue to spread the word of the superiority of God over all other beings and powers, no matter how much Satan may tempt us to accept his lies. The Lord's church is part of God's plan to protect us from those lies.

I recall hearing many years ago about some missionary activities in Africa. There were two different missionary groups, with two different approaches to their mission efforts. One group taught people about Christ and made a point of establishing churches. They encouraged the converts to be active in the church. The other group also taught the people about Christ, but they did not emphasize the importance of the church. Years later, someone did a follow-up study. Those who had been urged to be active in the church still assembled together and still worked for the Lord. But the people who had not attended church regularly could not be found. They had given up and gone back to their old ways.

God's plan was that Christians should band together in the church to withstand evil. There is strength in numbers; therefore, we are stronger when we do not have to stand alone. Satan knows that if he can keep us away from other Christians, he can more easily control us. He is aware of the saying "divide and conquer," and he uses it effectively. Thus we are better protected from Satan when we are constant in attendance in the Lord's church and active in the work of the Lord. A week without worshipping the Lord with fellow Christians leaves us weak. His love protects us best when we do not wander off, but remain close to him.

Paul's Prayer

Paul prayed for the Ephesians:

> I pray that, according to the riches of his glory, he may grant that you may be strengthened in your inner being with power through his Spirit, and that Christ may dwell in your hearts through faith, as you are being rooted and grounded in love. I pray that you may have the power to comprehend, with all the saints, what is the breadth and length and height and depth, and to know the love of Christ that surpasses knowledge, so that you may be filled with all the fullness of God. (Eph. 3:16–19 NRSV).

Absolutely nothing can separate us from the love of Christ (Rom. 8:35). His love for us surpasses knowledge. We cannot explain it because we cannot understand it. How can we understand a love so much deeper and so much more all-encompassing than any human love could possibly be? It is truly awe-inspiring! However, the more we are exposed to that love, and the more we read about it in Scripture and experience it in our lives, the more we will begin to glimpse a little of the glory of that love.

Jesus loves us so much that he prayed that his father would protect his disciples even as Jesus himself protected them while he was on earth (John 17:11–12): "My prayer is not that you take them out of the world but that you protect them from the evil one" (v. 15). Jesus intended that this protection would extend to future generations of disciples: "My prayer is not for them alone. I pray also for those who will believe in me through their message" (v. 20). And Jesus, the Messiah, is the giver of that love, and he is everywhere in the universe: "He who descended is the very one who ascended higher than all the heavens, in order to fill the whole universe" (Eph. 4:10). Because he fills the universe, there is nowhere in the whole universe that he is not present. He is always with us no matter where we go. The fact that Jesus is everywhere is another difficult concept for us to grasp. We just must accept it. We must have faith that it is true.

Paul closes his prayer by offering praise to God for his mighty power, and to show that he is glorified in the church: "Now to him who is able to do immeasurably more than all we ask or imagine, according to his power that is at work within us, to him be glory in the church and in Christ Jesus throughout all generations, for ever and ever! Amen" (Eph.3:20-21). The same power that raised Christ from the dead (Eph. 1:20) is available to us.

Our human minds cannot even imagine how great the power of God is and what he can do through us. It is awesome that God makes that power available to us! It is only with the help of God's mighty power that we are able to stand against the evil in this world.

Paul's Plea to the Ephesians

Because of the infinite power and wisdom of God, Paul makes a plea to the Ephesians: "So I tell you this, and insist on it in the Lord, that you must no longer live as the Gentiles do, in the futility of their thinking. They are darkened in their understanding and separated from the life of God because of the ignorance that is in them due to the hardening of their hearts" (Eph. 4:17-18). Separated from the life of God. This is a good description of our society today, isn't it? This is what was mentioned at the beginning of this chapter—the evil that is all around us. The minds of those who are alienated from God are closed. With closed minds, they cannot learn about the blessings and love that God lavishes on those who are his children. But Paul urges the Ephesians, and us, to change from the sinful way of life to the way of life that is in God's likeness: "You were taught, with regard to your former way of life, to put off your old self, which is being corrupted by its deceitful desires; to be made new in the attitude of your minds; and to put on the new self, created to be like God in true righteousness and holiness" (Eph. 4:22-24).

We cannot continue to live in sin and expect God to protect us (Rom. 6:1-2). We must renounce sin and try to live in God's likeness. God calls us to live upright and godly lives. He wants us to do what is right in every circumstance. It makes no difference if someone is watching us or not. The actions of an upright person will be the same in public and in private. Have you ever been given too much change at a store? What did you do? Keep the money and rejoice that no one except you knew about it? Or did you return the money to its rightful owner? We never know who is watching us, so we should do the right thing even when we think we are alone. Of course, we are never alone—God is always with us. When we are trying to live a devout life, we will put God first and will not let anything hinder our doing what is right.

When we sin, it allows the devil into our lives—it allows him to get past our protection. Paul admonishes us in Ephesians 4:27: "and do not give the devil a foothold." Even if no one else knows of our sins, God knows and he mourns. The devil knows, and he rejoices as he gets his foot in the door of our lives. We must be consistent in resisting the devil.

The way to avoid sin is to try to be like God: "Be imitators of God, therefore, as dearly loved children and live a life of love, just as Christ loved us and gave himself up for us as a fragrant offering and sacrifice to God" (Eph. 5:1–2). The way to be upright and devout is to be imitators of God. We are his dearly loved children, and he is our loving father. Of course we should try to be like him! God is love, and when we live in love, we become more like him. God is love, and Christ loved us enough to die for us; therefore we should return that love by imitating God.

Live in Love

Paul gives an explanation of what it means to live in love. In order to live this life of love we must follow God's will. Not only must we do what is pleasing to God, but we must avoid those things that are displeasing to him: "and find out what pleases the Lord. Have nothing to do with the fruitless deeds of darkness, but rather expose them" (Eph. 5:10–11). Evil deeds are all around us, and we need to recognize exactly what they are—fruitless deeds of darkness.

To live a life of love, we must avoid all things that displease God. We may think, "Well, I can go to this R-rated movie. It won't hurt me, I'm mature enough that it won't affect me adversely to see it." But we should remember that God said, "Have nothing to do with the fruitless deeds of darkness, but rather expose them" (Eph. 5:11). If we attend immoral events, we will be taking part in them, and our example may encourage a weaker believer to participate in the activity. Not only is it bad for us, but it also encourages immorality in our society. When the film makes money, more movies of that type are made. But it is not only immoral movies that we must avoid. We should also avoid such things as pornography on TV, on the internet, and in magazines. We need to be discerning about our entertainment. We need to "Avoid every kind of evil" (1 Thess. 5:22)—that is, we should avoid evil in whatever form it appears.

Perhaps we should ask ourselves, "Would I be embarrassed to be in this place if the Lord saw me going in? If I am there against his wishes, will he still protect me from the evil I choose to see?" Just remember, God does see everywhere you go. He is everywhere (Ps. 139:1–10). And also remember, you are the one who makes the choice: will you please God or not?

Because God's love transforms us from the dominion of darkness into his kingdom of light, we must try to please God in every way we can and grow and mature in his love. My prayer for you is the same as that of Paul for the Christians in Colosse:

> For this reason, since the day we heard about you, we have not stopped praying for you and asking God to fill you with the knowledge of his will through all spiritual wisdom and understanding. And we pray this in order that you may live a life worthy of the Lord and may please him in every way: bearing fruit in every good work, growing in the knowledge of God, being strengthened with all power according to his glorious might so that you may have great endurance and patience, and joyfully giving thanks to the Father, who has qualified you to share in

the inheritance of the saints in the kingdom of light. For he has rescued us from the dominion of darkness and brought us into the kingdom of the Son he loves, in whom we have redemption, the forgiveness of sins. (Col. 1:9–14)

———————FOR FURTHER THOUGHT———————

1. In what ways have you been made aware of the love of the Lord?

2. What passages of Scripture tell us that Satan is still active today?

3. Paul says that God has given us "every spiritual blessing in Christ." What are some spiritual blessings that are especially important to you?

4. What are some ways in which you have been aware of God's mighty power in your life?

5. How has God's wisdom been made known through the church? Why is the church important to us today? How important is the church to you?

CHAPTER FOUR

GOD'S LOVE PROTECTS

"The Lord will rescue me from every evil attack."
—2 TIMOTHY 4:18

In Ephesians 5:21–6:9, Paul gives instructions about how to act toward our fellow Christians, especially members of one's own household. Paul then turns to a discussion of protection against Satan. It is almost as if he has been building through the whole book to this climax—the passage quoted at the beginning of chapter three. We need the protection of God's armor.

Let us consider Ephesians 6:10–18 verse-by-verse.

"Finally, be strong in the Lord and in his mighty power." (v. 10)

It is important to notice that the emphasis in this passage is on the Lord and his power rather than on us and what we can do. Our strength must come from the Lord, because our puny strength is nothing compared to his mighty power. It is also nothing compared to the power of Satan. It is only through the power of the Lord that we have any protection against the devil.

"Put on the full armor of God so that you can take your stand against the devil's schemes." (v. 11)

God himself provides this armor out of his own arsenal. It is only his armor that enables us to stand firm when we are attacked by Satan. We should note that this armor is provided for our protection. It is defensive rather than offensive. God provides the armor so that we can stand our ground against Satan while God fights the battle.

A friend who had been going through some rough times recently said, "I know what Ephesians 6 says about putting on the whole armor of God, but sometimes I don't feel like a knight in shining armor—I feel more like a knight in battered armor." But he was looking at things from the wrong angle. He seemed to be trying to wear his own armor—something that he had provided for his own protection. When he tried to wear his own armor instead of God's, he did not receive the full benefit of the armor, and thus he felt battered. Often, we too make this mistake. But remember, it is God who provides the equipment. This is really God's own armor, not ours, but he makes it available to us. We may be reminded of the armor Saul provided for David (1 Sam. 17:38–40). Saul's armor did not help David; it did not fit him, nor was he accustomed to it. However, it is important to realize that the armor that God provides for us fits each of us perfectly. The more we use it, the more we become accustomed to it, and the more effective it is. Our inferior armor can be battered; God's perfect armor cannot. It is only by God's power that the devil can be defeated.

> "For our struggle is not against flesh and blood, but against the rulers, against the authorities, against the powers of this dark world and against the spiritual forces of evil in the heavenly realms." (v. 12)

We are struggling not against other people, but against Satan himself and all his superhuman powers. We see sinful people and are tempted to think that they are our enemies, so we want to destroy them. But that is wrong. By personalizing the battle, we detest the person instead of the sin. We must constantly remind ourselves that our enemy is Satan, not the sinful person. It is Satan who tempts not only that person but all of us to sin. It is a spiritual battle.

Make no mistake about it—the devil is alive and busy in our world today. Many people recognize Satan and talk admiringly about him and his power—some even openly worship him. We must recognize the fact that he really does exist and that he works overtime to corrupt God's people. He has had the ages to study humans and our weaknesses. He knows exactly how to tempt each one of us.[1]

We may think we are smart enough to protect ourselves against Satan, but we are not. Every time we think we have figured out how to resist him, he has already come up with another stratagem to tempt us. We are amateurs at withstanding his wiles, but God is a pro. Only God knows what Satan is up to and how to combat him. We must have God's help in order to survive.

Using God's armor is important, because the conflict is between God's kingdom and the devil's kingdom. It is not between heaven and earth, but between Good and Evil. This spiritual war is being fought out on the earth, but the forces of evil are no more confined to this world than are the forces of good. God is not the only spiritual force seeking to control our destiny, but he is the one whom we want to control it.

The armor referenced in Ephesians 6:10–18 is a mighty defense against the devil and all his ways. The battle is not against the people around us but against forces of evil that we cannot see, that we cannot comprehend. Because we fight "against the spiritual forces of evil in the heavenly realms" (v. 12), we need more than our own earthly abilities. Hence God lovingly provides us with his own armor and he fights Satan for us.

> "Therefore put on the full armor of God, so that when the day of evil comes, you may be able to stand your ground, and after you have done everything, to stand." (v. 13)

Again Paul says that this is God's armor, not ours. But we do have to take it up, to put it on, to use it. When we use his armor, God enables us to stand up against the devil. The only way we can withstand these evil forces is with the help of God's armor. We learn about that armor only when we open our Bibles, read the descriptions, and obey the commands concerning the armor. Only in the Bible do we find the essential user's manual.

The conflict with Satan is ongoing and persistent; it is ever being renewed. These verses do not refer merely to arming oneself—that is, getting ready to fight—but they include the constant, daily battle against evil. They indicate that we must accomplish this difficult task every day. Sometimes we feel so overwhelmed that we think there is no hope, no way out of the mire of worldliness. This is when we need God's protective armor the most. We have to realize that although we cannot do it by ourselves, God will help us when we do our best to stand against evil.

> "Stand firm then, with the belt of truth buckled around your waist." (v. 14a)

Paul uses the illustration of a soldier's armor in order to show us what we need from God's armor. The soldier's tunic was worn with a wide belt that not only held the loose garments close to his body so he could move quickly and unencumbered, but also held his sword. The belt of truth is what holds everything together so that the armor is effective for us.

Remember: this is God's armor, God's truth. The truth of the gospel, the truthfulness of God, all the eternal truths of the universe are available to us and support us. God and his truthfulness hold everything together. On the other side, Satan is the father of lies, and thus should not be believed, no matter how many times he repeats his evil ideas (all around us: in the movies, on TV, in music, sometimes even from our friends). Satan is the opposite of God. However, Satan trembles before the mighty truth that God exists (James 2:19). He knows the truth of everything that is revealed about God in the Bible. He knows that God is in control of the universe. The truth of God is what terrifies the devil. How blessed we are that God loves us enough to provide his truthfulness to protect us against the devil!

As we fasten on this belt of truth, we must be truthful in our lives because lies, or any kind of dishonesty, destroy the usefulness of the armor. Of course, I can stand firm and tell the truth all day long, and the devil in the midst of his realm may do nothing but laugh at my puny efforts, but wearing God's belt of truth obligates us to a life of seeking the truth and being truthful. Fortunately, because God knows that our own truthfulness is not enough, he supplies what we lack. We should praise God and thank him for the fact that this belt refers to his truthfulness, not to ours, and that he loves us enough to protect us with his truth.

"[W]ith the breastplate of righteousness in place." (v. 14b)

Some translations call it the "breastplate of righteousness." Others use the word "integrity." There is a close connection between righteousness and integrity. Both involve rightness and justice, and each helps to explain the meaning of the other. The breastplate defended the heart of the soldier.

Isaiah 59:15b–17a uses the same illustration of the breastplate and of the helmet:

> The Lord looked and was displeased
> that there was no justice.
> He saw that there was no one,
>   he was appalled that there was no one to intervene;
> so his own arm worked salvation for him,
>   and his own righteousness sustained him.
> He put on righteousness as his breastplate,
>   and the helmet of salvation on his head.

The breastplate is the righteousness, the uprightness of character, the integrity, that protects us from the assaults of evil. Notice that the breastplate in Isaiah, as in Ephesians, is God's righteousness. God alone is totally righteous and always acts with integrity. Thus it is his righteousness and integrity that provide the breastplate that defends our hearts. That is, it is really God's uprightness of character, integrity, and righteousness, not ours, that protect us. The breastplate of righteousness would not be much protection if it were only our own righteousness, which is too insignificant to be of any value against the assault of such an experienced warrior as the devil. He can easily get through to us if our only protection is our own integrity. But God is the holy one, the righteous one. It is his righteousness that we can hide behind. It is because of him that we even know the difference between right and wrong. It is only by trying to be like him that we can have any righteousness in our lives.

We need the perfection of God's total holiness, his total integrity, which is available to us, to protect us. No righteousness of our own could enable us to stand against the forces of evil. Our own integrity is no protection against accusations of conscience, whispers of despondency, and powers of temptation. We dare not trust in our own righteousness. Rather we trust in the infinitely perfect righteousness consisting in the obedience and suffering of Christ that satisfies the divine law and justice.

The "righteousness of God" is God's activity in making us righteous, which he does in Christ (2 Cor. 5:21; Phil. 3:8–9). God imparts his righteousness to us in Christ: "But now he has reconciled you by Christ's physical body through death to present you holy in his sight, without blemish and free from accusation" (Col. 1:22). Yet although it is the integrity and holiness of God that guard our hearts and keep us safe in the love of the Lord, that does not release any of us from the responsibility to live righteously. Each of us must put on the breastplate of righteousness and wear it. Each of us must do all we can to imitate God and be holy as he is holy (1 Pet. 1:15–16). Righteousness begins with justification, but it continues with the new, obedient life. Thus we have in verse 14 both the righteousness bestowed by God and our own living in righteousness.

> "[A]nd with your feet fitted with the readiness that come from the gospel of peace." (v. 15)

The gospel is ready to protect us from Satan. It is the source of whatever readiness we have. Preparation, or readiness, is itself the foot covering that keeps us from losing our footing. Again it is the gospel, something provided by God, and not our own preparation that protects our feet and equips us for battle. It is not our readiness to preach the gospel, but the fact that the gospel gives us the readiness, the preparation for sure-footedness. We need to do everything we can to be ready, to be prepared for our spiritual warfare. The ultimate preparation is to be equipped with the gospel of peace.

Perhaps a passage from Isaiah suggested to Paul the association between the gospel (or good news), the messenger bringing it, and feet:

> How beautiful on the mountains
> > are the feet of those who bring good news,
> who proclaim peace,
> > who bring good tidings,
> > who proclaim salvation. (Isa. 52:7)

The gospel is the message of peace. This peace is what the Lord provides for us even in the midst of a battle. Peace in the middle of warfare is a paradox that we cannot fully comprehend: it is the "peace of God, which transcends all understanding" (Phil. 4:7). It is a feeling of calmness and courage. It is the assurance of God's ultimate victory. Peace in the heart shows itself in the readiness of the feet. Our peace with God makes us eager for the fight with Satan.

If we try to achieve any peace other than that of God's gospel, we will not have the firm footing that we need. We cannot assume that we can make peace with Satan by ignoring him and pretending that he does not exist so that we do not have to contend with him. That so-called peace will only bring more trouble, not protection. The very fact that we must be ready implies that we are preparing to do something. We cannot sit idly by and let Satan's lies continue to spread all through our society. We have to do what we can to spread the gospel in order to counteract the forces of evil. If we do not tell others the Good News, then they may never hear it. If they do not hear it, they cannot obey it, and then Satan will have won more souls.

As we have our "feet fitted with the readiness that comes from the gospel of peace," it is the Good News of Christ that will enable us to be ready to meet the devil and defeat him. Christ has already won the final, decisive victory over Satan by his death, burial, and resurrection. But there are still battles that must be fought—Satan does not give up easily. We can overcome the evil one only because of the actions of Christ. Because of him and what he has done for us, there will ultimately be peace and an end to the warfare. This is the gospel of peace.

> "In addition to all this, take up the shield of faith, with which you can extinguish all the flaming arrows of the evil one." (v. 16)

In ancient warfare, arrows were set on fire and shot toward the enemy. Shields were often made of wood covered with leather and soaked in water. When the arrow stuck in the shield, the arrow's fire would be put out.

The shield was a very important element in Roman armor. As the soldiers advanced in close ranks, the shields would be held in front of each one in the line of soldiers, thus making a solid front. Arrows could only penetrate where there were gaps—where someone was not doing his assigned job. The second row of soldiers held their shields above their heads and the heads of those in the front line. This formed something like an umbrella that protected against the long-range flaming arrows.

The shield of faith is very important to us, too. The Greek word "faith" could be used in several ways. Among other meanings, it could refer to the facts about God revealed in the Bible. This seems to be the primary meaning here. It is the Faith, the facts in which we must believe, that will put out the burning arrows of Satan. If we put our faith in anything less than the facts revealed in the Bible about God and his infinite power and love, then our faith is in vain and will not protect us against Satan. Our faith is never perfect, but the one in whom we believe is perfect. We believe in God because of who he is and what he has done.

The Greek word "faith" can also mean "faithfulness." God himself is the only being or power that is completely faithful, who always does what is right and just and holy. The shield of faith would not be strong enough if it depended merely upon our faith. We must rely on God's power and love to protect us against the evil forces in the universe, and we must recognize the faithfulness of God. He is always in power. We are his children, and as a loving parent, he is always there for us, to love us, to protect us, to shield us from the evil powers that attack us. It is only on his faithfulness that we can rely, and it is only him in whom we can have faith.

Whether we think of this shield as the facts of the gospel, faith in God himself, or the faithfulness of God, it is still a part of God's own armor. To be most effective, this faith should include all three aspects.

When we believe in the power of God's shield of faith, we will utilize it in our battles against Satan. However, it is not enough merely to say, "I believe." The fiery darts of the Devil are not quenched until we confess what we believe. We need to tell others what we believe and why.

The teenage daughter of a friend was in a high school English class studying the beatitudes as literature. The teacher said, "We all know that this is only a myth, but it is great literature and as such it is worth reading."

The girl did not agree with the teacher's comment, so she raised her hand and respectfully told the teacher, "You may think the Bible is a myth, but I believe with my whole heart that it is the word of God and that it is true. I would stake my life on it."

Later several classmates told her how glad they were that she had the courage to speak up for the truth. They admitted that they had been too timid.

It took courage for this girl to speak up to her teacher. It also takes courage for us to stand up to Satan and tell him of our belief in the Lord. But we should be like that young girl and always be ready to tell others about our faith. We prepare for that by studying God's word, which is where we learn what to believe. We also find the courage to stand up for our faith because of the assurance that God is with us when we tell others what we believe. We need to speak up without being ashamed. We should know the Bible so well that we are always ready to quote pertinent Scripture to tell others about our faith and hope (1 Pet. 3:15).

Remember how Jesus responded when he was tempted by the devil after his baptism (Matt. 4:1–11)? After each temptation, Jesus said, "It is written." Then he quoted scriptures, and those scriptures disarmed the devil. In the same way, we must hold up to the devil not merely our believing or our subjective faith, but the Faith, the Word, the Doctrine, the pertinent Scripture passage, the objective content of faith. You may believe something with all your might but that will not necessarily be a quenching shield. Everything depends on what you believe and in whom you believe. Of course, we must believe these things wholeheartedly, totally relying on their truth and power.

"Take the helmet of salvation." (v. 17a)

The helmet protects the center of physical life just as God's salvation provides for our eternal life. Paul is not speaking of what the believer does to save himself, but of the salvation itself that comes from God. However, we must take up God's helmet of salvation on his terms. Our own assurance would be empty if the reality wasn't there. What a magnificent blessing that he loves us enough to provide his own helmet for our protection!

"[A]nd the sword of the Spirit, which is the word of God." (v. 17b)

Although the sword is the part of the armor that attacks, it is mainly defensive rather than offensive. The Greek word used here refers to a small sword, something like a dagger. The Christian has access to the sword, which is the word of God, as identified both here and in Revelation 1:16: "In his right hand he held seven stars, and out of his mouth came a sharp double-edged sword."

We find that the words of God in the Bible are both defensive and offensive. It is there that we find the words that comfort us, the words that show us how to live our lives and how to protect ourselves against evil. It is also there that we find the words to persuade sinners to repent and obey God's commands, thus taking a precious soul away from Satan. When we use the word of God as a sword in battle, we are to use it as God's utterance. Any change we make in what God says takes the edge off the sword and removes its power. We must have a weapon that will crush spiritual forces. No words of ours, however brilliant, can influence Satan. But the word of the Lord God himself, the sword of the Spirit through which he acts, is powerful to defeat the devil.

Without the word of God, we could not make an attack on evil. Any soldier is doomed if all his weapons are defensive and none are offensive. We must have God's own words that reveal him and his character, his nature, his very being. Otherwise we have nothing to use in a counterattack against the evil around us. It is with God's words that we can show the difference between right and wrong and persuade others that God's way is best, and it is only in the Bible that we find God's words. Therefore, we must study our Bibles faithfully.

> "And pray in the Spirit on all occasions with all kinds of prayers and requests. With this in mind, be alert and always keep on praying for all the saints." (v. 18)

It is not the armor or weapons alone that make the warrior; there must be courage and strength also. Prayer links the Christian with the strength of the Lord. Prayer is naturally connected with action. We need spiritual help to fight a spiritual battle. Without prayer, none of God's armor would be available to us.

The combatant, even in the stress of personal conflict, thinks of all those with whom he is united. We do not stand by ourselves; we stand with all of God's people. In this way, even the weakest saint can have a part in the fight against Satan. It has been said that "Satan trembles when he sees even the weakest saint on his knees."

We should remember that prayer is our lifeline to God. It is essential that we stay in constant contact with that lifeline (1 Thess. 5:17).

The Christian's Uniform

The ancient soldier had his armor, or uniform. In like manner, modern soldiers are issued uniforms upon entering the military. It is important for soldiers to wear their uniforms so that others can see that they are in service to the country of which they are citizens.

In the same way, Christians have uniforms. The citizenship of Christians is not on the earth, but in heaven (Phil. 3:20). Therefore Christians have heavenly uniforms. These uniforms give much greater protection to the Christians than the Roman armor gave to Rome's soldiers. Christians are given this superior uniform when they are baptized and thus become a part of service to the Lord. The Christian's uniform is even more important for protection than the Roman's armor because the Roman soldier is clothed only with armor, but the Christian is clothed with Christ: "For all of you who were baptized into Christ have clothed yourselves with Christ" (Gal.3:27; see also Rom. 13:14).

Being clothed with Christ means that when God looks at us, he sees only Christ, not our sinfulness. That is the only way he can consider us to be holy and without blemish in his sight (Col. 1:21–23). What greater protection can we have than that? And what great love God has for us to provide us with this protection!

Conclusion

As we try to live for the love of the Lord, we must incorporate all the parts of armor into our lives. However, we must remember that it is the armor of God, not of ourselves, that will protect us from Satan. God provides us with perfect armor and a perfect sword, but it is up to us to learn to use them in the best ways possible.

If a soldier is left to his own defenses, he will be in a precarious position. That which is given to him to fight the battles will be stronger and better than that which he could provide for himself. So it is with our spiritual warfare. God gives us the armor that we need, and it is his mighty armor, not our own puny defenses.

The emphasis of Ephesians 6:10–18 and of this chapter has been on what God provides for our protection. The armor is God's, and the clothing we wear is Christ. Lest we draw the mistaken conclusion that there is little or nothing for us to do, that God does it all, remember that we have to put on the armor that God supplies and we must put on Christ in baptism. Paul emphasizes our part by repeated reference to what we must do. A literal translation of these verses includes: "Put on the armor" (6:11); "Take up the armor" (6:13); "Gird yourself with the belt" (6:14); "Shod your feet" (6:15); "Take up the shield" (6:16); "Receive the helmet and sword" (6:17).

Because God loves us, we do not need to do it all ourselves. We can draw on his strength. We are not alone in our battle to live for the love of the Lord, to live uprightly in the face of the evil around us. It is because God loves us that he protects us with his own armor and with his own son. We must put that armor on and go out to do our daily battles. We must live our lives in imitation of Christ (Eph. 5:1–2).

It has been said, "There is not enough darkness in the whole world to put out the light of one single candle." Neither is there enough evil in the world to put out the goodness of one small child of God.

This chapter started on a note of despondency and fear, but it ends on a note of hope, of courage, of dependence on the almighty God and his wisdom and power and love. Philippians 4:13 says, "I can do everything through him who gives me strength." It is awesome to realize this truth: God is on our side.

As I think about the magnitude of what he does for us, I am reminded of Jesus's prayer in John 17, and my heart soars in a prayer of gratitude that God answers this prayer:

"I will remain in the world no longer, but they are still in the world, and I am coming to you. Holy Father, protect them by the power of your name—the name you gave me—so that they may be one as we are one. While I was with them, I protected them and kept them safe by that name you gave me. . . . My prayer is not that you take them out of the world but that you protect them from the evil one." (v. 11–12, 15)

---FOR FURTHER THOUGHT---

1. Which part of God's armor is most important to you and why?

2. Ephesians 6:11 says to "put on the full armor of God." How can you do this?

3. How does Philippians 4:13 affect your daily life?

4. Give illustrations of how the sword can be used both defensively and offensively.

CHAPTER FIVE

LOVE AND MARRIAGE

"Marriage should be honored by all."
—HEBREWS 13:4

Marriage is God's idea, his plan for humanity: "The Lord God said, 'It is not good for the man to be alone. I will make a helper suitable for him'" (Gen. 2:18). So God created woman and ordained marriage: "For this reason a man will leave his father and mother and be united to his wife, and they will become one flesh" (Gen. 2:24).

God made us and therefore knows everything about us. He knows what is best for us. He knows what will make our marriages what they should be. He knows what will make us joyful and what will help us to lead full, rich lives. He also knows that the only way for us to be truly happy is to be holy. And the only way to be holy is to follow God's will. If we follow his plan for our lives, we will be what he wants us to be, and our marriages will be more meaningful, more satisfying. The closer we are to God, the more joy we will experience.

The joy that God means when he says, "Rejoice in the Lord always" (Phil. 4:4) is not a joy that is cheerful and laughing all the time. It is the deep-down knowledge that God is with you and you are doing his will. It is having the proper reverence for God and his majesty and recognizing his great power. It is doing right for the love of the Lord:

> Better a little with the fear of the Lord
> than great wealth with turmoil.

> Better a meal of vegetables where there is love
> than a fattened calf with hatred. (Prov. 15:16–17)

Proverbs 16:3 reminds us how important it is to pray about everything. If we want our marriages to be successful, we must rely on God in all our plans:

> Commit to the Lord whatever you do,
> and your plans will succeed.

It is my prayer that your life, and especially your marriage, will be enriched by considering the passages of Scripture that deal with social relationships, especially between husbands and wives. These verses may be very familiar to you, but it will be good to study them again, trying to get fresh insights that we can apply to our daily lives. May we follow God's plan in everything.

God planned that we show our love for him by obedience to his wishes. Thus, when he gives us instructions about marriage, we show our love for the Lord by obeying those plans that he has made for us from the beginning of time.

Many people have written their own versions of "The Ten Commandments of Love," or "12 Rules for a Happy Marriage," or other such lists. But let us see what God has said will build better relationships between husbands and wives, and indeed between others as well, because God's ways are always best. Some of the following passages of Scripture deal primarily with marriage, and some deal with other relationships. However, they all tell us something important that will help our marriages to be more meaningful.

Rule #1

"But seek first his kingdom and his righteousness, and all these things will be given to you as well" (Matt. 6:33).

Get your priorities right. In everything put God first. Live according to the principles he has set forth in the Bible. Study the Bible together, pray together, go to church together, serve God together. If you have children, include them in your daily devotional times. Train them to love God and his word. Strengthen your faith daily. Learn to rely on God, to trust him in everything. Do everything in your power to see that you and your family will go to heaven: "Live in such a way that God's love can bless you as you wait for the eternal life that our Lord Jesus Christ in his mercy is going to give you" (Jude 21 NLT).

Recognize the importance of being spiritually minded as you put first things first. Perhaps you have seen a demonstration with rocks, gravel, sand, and a jar. If the sand and small rocks (which represent the things in our lives on which we spend our time) are put into the jar first, then there is no room for the large rocks (which represent the time we spend with the Lord). But if the big rocks are put in first, the small rocks next, and finally the sand, there is room for everything. When we put God first, then we have time for other things in our lives. But if we put other things first, then we find that there is no time left over for God.

Perhaps you have heard it said that "I am too busy not to pray." This means that we need to put prayer in that jar before we try to put in all the things that keep us busy. When we spend time in prayer with God, our lives go more smoothly. It is especially important to pray when we are busy, because we need God's help to get through each day.

Remember that God's way is always the best way, therefore find out what his will is and follow it with your whole heart. Be righteous in all that you do so that you will prosper:

> The Lord's curse is on the house of the wicked,
> but he blesses the home of the righteous. (Prov. 3:33)

Rule #2

"Therefore shall a man leave his father and his mother, and shall cleave unto his wife: and they shall be one flesh" (Gen. 2:24 KJV).

It is important that newlyweds make their own family unit. Of course, they should not ignore their parents, but their first allegiance should be to each other. The King James translation says that a man will "leave" his parents and "cleave" to his wife. That is, they will cling to each other; they will make their own family unit and become independent of their parents. This new family will be more important to them than their families of origin.

In many wedding ceremonies, candles are used to symbolize the making of a new family. The bride's parents light one candle and the groom's parents light another. Then later in the ceremony, the bride and groom take those candles and use them together to light a larger candle. Then they blow out the candles lit by their parents. This illustrates the transition they are making from their parents' families to their own new family.

It is important for the parents of the new couple to recognize that there is a new family unit, and that their roles have changed. A lady in Canada once told me that the best advice she ever received on being a mother-in-law was to keep her arms open and her mouth shut.

Part of cleaving to each other is spending time together. Relationships can grow only when there is togetherness. It takes time to build the close ties that make a good marriage. Put the marriage ahead of any individuals in the family. What is good for the marriage is good for everyone in it, including the children. Let the children see your love for each other.

Another part of cleaving is commitment. It is important to keep any promise that one makes, but it is essential to keep the marriage vows. God instituted marriage, and he hears the promises made at the wedding. In fact, it is he who joins the two into one in their new relationship:

> "Haven't you read," [Jesus] replied, "that at the beginning the Creator made them male and female, and said, 'For this reason a man will leave his father and mother and be united to his wife, and the two will become one flesh'? So they are no longer two, but one. Therefore what God has joined together, let man not separate." (Matt. 19:4–6)

We must take very seriously the promises we make at our weddings. We must be totally committed to keeping our vows and making the marriage what it should be. God is the one who joins the husband and wife in marriage, and he does not want the marriage vows to be broken (Matt. 19:6; Mal. 2:16).

Therefore both the husband and the wife should make every effort to keep the marriage vows and to make the marriage as good as possible. They should cultivate the love they felt when they were courting and not let that love die. There is always room for improvement in the marriage relationship, and each couple must try to follow what God wants for them— that is, to have a holy, happy marriage, according to his plans.

Rule #3
"[E]ach one ... must love his wife ... the wife must respect her husband" (Eph. 5:33).

Husbands are commanded to love their wives with agape love. That is, the husband should put his wife and her needs ahead of his own, using the same kind of sacrificial love that Jesus has for all of us (Eph 5:25). The husband should make a conscious decision to love his wife and then treat her lovingly.

The command to husbands to love their wives as Christ loved the church is more difficult to follow than the command to wives in verses 22-24, 33. If a man truly follows this command, he will be ready to die before allowing any harm to come to his wife. Obviously, that includes harm from the husband himself. Anyone who follows God's command to love his wife cannot be abusive to her.

A different Greek word is used in Titus 2:4 for the love a woman should have for her husband. That word is a form of *phileo*, which emphasizes the idea of fondness or affection. This is love that involves respect and tender, caring feelings. This kind of love can be learned, according to Titus 2:4. The older women "can train the younger women to love their husbands and children." This kind of love takes time to develop. One way to learn to love in this way is by doing the right actions and having the right attitudes toward the husband. As the wife acts in a kindly, loving way toward her husband, the feelings of tenderness and caring will become stronger.

Husbands and wives both need to know that they have the complete love of their spouses. One chooses to love in this way rather than merely doing whatever feels good. It is not enough to say that you love someone (1 John 3:18); you must act on that love. This kind of love can be directed even to someone you do not like (Matt. 5:44) and to someone who is very unlovable (Rom. 5:7–8). It is the love that a husband has for his wife even if he has "fallen out of love with" her. No matter how he feels toward her, he still must treat her as lovingly as Christ does the church.

God and Jesus shower love upon us daily, and we learn how to love by paying attention to how God shows his love. For instance, one blessing of his love for us is that he always listens to our prayers. Thus, if husbands love their wives in the way God loves us, they will listen carefully to their wives and pay attention to what they are saying. The same is true of wives. Husbands need to have someone to listen carefully to them just as surely as wives do.

Love, *agape* love, puts the other person first and is not selfish or self-serving. Selfishness and happiness cannot co-exist. There is no room for selfishness in a loving relationship. Again, you cannot force someone to feel love for you, but by treating that person in a loving manner, the love that you desire will most likely follow.

I am reminded of a story I once heard. Whether it is true or not, I do not know, but I do know that it rings true to experience. A woman had decided that she no longer loved her husband. She was so angry with him that she wanted to hurt him as much as she possibly could. She went to a divorce lawyer and asked for advice. He said: "If you really want to hurt him, do this: For the next few months act toward him as you did when you were first courting. Make him think you love him dearly; then when you file for divorce, the shock and hurt will be even greater. It will destroy him. Come back to see me in six months, and we'll start the process."

She did exactly as he said. She still no longer felt any love for her husband, but she cooked his favorite meals for him, made sure his laundry was done exactly the way he liked it, spoke lovingly to him, did everything she could think of that he especially liked. She showered him with loving attention. After six months of this, she saw the lawyer again. He said: "Okay, I'm ready to file the papers. If your husband has been led to believe you still love him, this divorce should really hurt him."

The woman replied: "But you don't understand. The last few months have been so wonderful that we have fallen in love all over again! As I did nice things for him, he began to notice and then he started doing nice things for me. I love him now more than ever and I no longer want a divorce!"

This woman made the decision to exercise agape love toward her husband. As she acted lovingly, her feelings of affection followed. When you want to get closer to someone, do loving things for that person, whether that person is lovable or not. Remember to pray for that person and for the relationship between the two of you.

1 Corinthians 7:1–7 is another important passage for husband-wife relationships. The sexual aspect of marriage is God-given and thus good. And it can be a beautiful experience. When each partner realizes that his or her body also belongs to the other, and that sexual intercourse is intended by God to bring pleasure to each other, love and respect will become more meaningful. So one should never withhold sexual favors to manipulate the other: "Do not deprive each other except by mutual consent" (1 Cor. 7:5). God gave us our sexual drives. Fulfilling those desires is an important part of loving each other but should be done only within God's holy plans for marriage.

Rule #4

"Submit to one another out of reverence for Christ. Wives, submit to your husbands, as to the Lord" (Eph. 5:21–22; see also Col. 3:18).
Society today seems to think that submission in any form is degrading. However, if one understands what the Bible means by submission, it is a

positive action, not detrimental to anyone. Biblical submission is a voluntary placing of oneself under the authority of another. It cannot be forced on the wife by the husband. And, contrary to popular opinion, the woman is to submit only to her own husband, not to all men.

The Greek word "submit" is used in the New Testament thirty-eight times, but only six of those refer to a woman being in submission to her husband.[1] The rest of the references to submission involve a number of different groups. Angels, authorities, and powers are in submission to Christ (1 Pet. 3:21–22); every person must submit to God (James 4:7); Christ submits to God (Heb. 5:7–8); Christians submit to political powers (Titus 3:1); the church submits to Christ (Eph. 1:22–23); Christians submit to church leaders (1 Cor. 16:15–16); younger people should submit to the older (1 Pet. 5:5–6); and Christians must submit to one another (Eph. 5:21).

"What a man desires is unfailing love," Proverbs 19:22 tells us. The New Revised Standard Version translates that verse: "What is desirable in a person is loyalty."[2] Unfailing love equals loyalty. One way that a wife shows love and loyalty to her husband is by her submission to him. She shows submission in having respect for him, among other ways. The wife should have the same respect for her husband that she wants for herself. She should also have respect for the work that he does. A man's job will sometimes take him away from home, but he needs to know that his wife respects and encourages him in his work. Likewise, the husband should show respect for his wife and what she does.

Part of treating someone with respect is using company manners at home. There is no place for rudeness in a loving home. "Please" and "Thank you" (among other courtesies) should be used often each day.

Although wives are commanded to submit to their own husbands, Ephesians 5:21 also says, "Submit to one another out of reverence for Christ." This involves a mutual submission. There are times when the husband must submit to the wife's wishes. The husband and wife should be mutually interdependent. Each should lift up the other. They should be a team, depending on each other for support and love. The husband must not be a tyrannical dictator; he must not "lord it over" his wife.

Submission does not mean that one swallows up the other. Each should have his or her own life and neither should try to run the other's life. Do not try to tell the other what to do and how to do it. Give each other space—do not crowd each other. Enjoy doing things together, and enjoy doing things separately. It is important to have mutual interests as well as individual interests. Cultivate the ability to appreciate and encourage one another. Do not become jealous of the other's accomplishments.

When one understands what the Lord means by submission and lives according to his will, it leads to the beautiful relationship between husband and wife that God planned for us.

Rule #5
"Marriage should be honored by all, and the marriage bed kept pure, for God will judge the adulterer and all the sexually immoral" (Heb. 13:4).

It is important to be faithful to each other (Proverbs 2:12–19; 5:15–23; and 6:23–29, 32). Being faithful to one's spouse involves both avoiding an extramarital affair and continuing to show that spouse proper love, including sexual love (1 Cor. 7:2–5).

In describing the kind of man who should be selected as an elder, 1 Timothy 3 and Titus 1 state that such a man must be the husband of one wife (literally "a one-woman man"). Titus 1:8 also states that he should be "disciplined." The Greek word used here is often translated "self-controlled" and it especially relates to sexual self-control. In other words, he must be a man who is completely faithful to his own wife; other women will have no fear of his ever making improper advances toward them. Although these two passages list qualities an elder in the Lord's church should have, most of these items are qualities which every Christian man should cultivate.

It is important for the husband to be faithful to his wife, and it is just as important for the wife to be faithful to her husband in all things. There is no room in the marriage relationship for a third party. A third party often leads to a divorce, and Malachi 2:16-17 tells us: "I hate divorce, says the Lord God of Israel, ... So guard yourself ... and do not break faith." Jesus, too, taught that divorce was not part of God's original plan for humans, although it had been allowed in certain circumstances under the old law: "Jesus replied, 'Moses permitted you to divorce your wives because your hearts were hard. But it was not this way from the beginning. I tell you that anyone who divorces his wife, except for marital unfaithfulness, and marries another woman commits adultery'" (Matt. 19:8-9).

Unfortunately, divorce and adultery are widely accepted in the world today. But Christians should do all they can to make their marriages what God wants them to be. The marriage vows include the promise to love and honor each other until death separates them. Both men and women need to live up to those vows. Total commitment to each other is an important part of every marriage.

Rule #6
"Honor one another above yourselves" (Rom. 12:10b).

To honor your spouse, tell others what a wonderful person he or she is. Build your partner up in the eyes of your friends. Let others know of your love and admiration. Tell the good things your spouse does. Compliment each other, especially in front of the children, thereby teaching them to respect their parents. Love each other by giving help and support. Trust each other.

> Criticizing or belittling your spouse in front of others hurts deeply:
> Reckless words pierce like a sword. (Prov. 12:18)

and

> Like a gold ring in a pig's snout
> is a beautiful woman who shows no discretion. (Prov. 11:22)

So when you see a fault in your spouse, don't spread it abroad—let others find out for themselves.

We all need to know that we are appreciated. Be aware of what your spouse does and thank him or her frequently. Does she have a good meal on the table at the right time? Thank her for it, whether it is what she usually does or if it is the first time in a week! Did he take out the trash without being asked? Thank him for it. Praise the good things your spouse does, even when you both consider those things to be normal tasks to be done daily without questioning or complaining.

Find something positive, something complimentary, to say to your spouse every day. Tell your spouse often, "I am so glad I married you!" And mean it. And of course, frequently tell your spouse, "I love you." Love is very important in a marriage. It must be renewed every day to be kept alive.

Paul tells husbands to love their wives in the same way that Christ loves the church. That is a tall order for any man, but it is an important command to all men (Eph. 5:25, 33). As the husband loves his wife and the wife respects her husband, their love will grow deeper and more meaningful as the years slip by. The mature love is even better than the "puppy love" they felt during courtship.

My prayer for you is that you may aspire to understand and live by the principles stated by Paul concerning marriage:

> Wives, submit to your husbands as to the Lord. For the husband is the head of the wife as Christ is the head of the church, his body, of which he is the Savior. Now as the church submits to Christ, so also wives should submit to their husbands in everything.
>
> Husbands, love your wives, just as Christ loved the church and gave himself up for her.... In the same way, husbands ought to love their wives as their own bodies. He who loves his wife loves himself. After all, no one ever hated his own body, but he feeds and cares for it, just as Christ does the church—for we are

members of his body. For this reason a man will leave his father and mother and be united to his wife, and the two will become one flesh. This is a profound mystery—but I am talking about Christ and the church. However, each one of you also must love his wife as he loves himself, and the wife must respect her husband. (Eph. 5:22–25, 28–33)

---FOR FURTHER THOUGHT---

1. Why do you think putting God first is important in a marriage?

2. What are some suggestions you have for making a new family when a couple marries?

3. What can a married couple do to keep alive the love they shared as they were courting?

4. Why do you think that many people, both in the world and in the church, think that submission is out-of-date and something to be avoided? Why do you think God commanded it?

5. What are some ways that husbands and wives can honor each other?

CHAPTER SIX

LOVE MAKES MARRIAGE MORE MEANINGFUL

"It is not good for the man to be alone."
—GENESIS 2:18

In the previous chapter, we considered a few rules or suggestions that will help us to make our marriages more meaningful. There are many others that we could contemplate, as well, but we cannot cover everything that will be meaningful in these short chapters. The limitation of print leaves you with the opportunity to think of other rules and suggestions that will be especially helpful to you. As we go along, you can make your own list by expanding on this one, and resolve to live by it.

RULE #7
"So in everything, do to others what you would have them do to you" (Matt. 7:12).

Jesus stated what we call the Golden Rule in his Sermon on the Mount (see Matt. 5–7). This teaching sums up and explains all that Jesus has been saying earlier in that passage. For example, a woman should be very careful about judging her husband, or anyone else. She must treat her husband the way she would like to be treated. Or, suppose a boy is hungry and asks his daddy for some food. The daddy will give it to him because he would like for someone to give him food when he is hungry. He would never give his child a rock to eat when the boy asked for some bread. So, even sinful human beings know how to give good gifts to their children and their spouses. And if that is true, Jesus says, we should think about how much better the gifts are that God gives his children when we ask (see 7:9–11).

When we do to others what we want them to do to us, we are living a life of love. Or, to put it as Jesus did, the Golden Rule sums up the Law and the Prophets (Matt. 7:12). With this assertion, Jesus was emphasizing how important the Golden Rule really is.

The Golden Rule involves caring concern for the other person. It means treating that person in a kind, loving way. And that is exactly what is important in a marriage: two people who treat each other the way they should. None of us likes to be treated harshly, so we should not treat our spouses harshly. Each of us likes to be treated fairly, so we should treat our spouses fairly. We should treat our spouses the way we like to be treated.

In Matthew 7:7–8, Jesus tells us to ask and the door will be opened for us. So we should always remember to talk to our father in heaven and ask him for what we need. He wants us to communicate with him.

We also need to learn to communicate with our spouses, because there are some situations in which communication is essential in knowing how to apply the Golden Rule. This was a lesson learned the hard way by a young couple. Not long after they married, the wife became ill. Her husband was at home, but he left her alone so she could rest. Sometime later, he was ill and she kept going into the bedroom to see if he needed anything, or if there was anything she could do for him.

Only later, after they had communicated with each other their attitudes toward illness, did they realize the truth. When she was ill, she was disappointed that he left her alone. What she really wanted was for someone to give her a lot of attention and to see her through her sickness with tender loving care. After all, that's what her mother always did for her. She wanted to be petted during her illness, but her husband wanted to be left alone. He did not want her to keep coming into the bedroom and disturbing him when he was ill.

Each was following the Golden Rule by doing to the other what he or she wanted when ill, but it was not working. Until they communicated their wishes to each other, it was difficult for them to follow the Golden Rule. It was important for each to learn what pleased the other one. Now that this couple has discussed their preferences, they treat each other's illnesses with understanding and compassion. And that is what the Golden Rule is about—doing what is right for the other person.

In some circumstances, we may wish to paraphrase the rule to say, "Do unto others what they would like for you to do for them."

Understanding and properly applying the Golden Rule is as important in marriage as in other relationships.

Rule #8
"Starting a quarrel is like breaching a dam; so drop the matter before a dispute breaks out" (Prov. 17:14).

Many passages in Proverbs speak to the problem of quarreling. Examples include:

> Starting a quarrel is like breaching a dam;
> so drop the matter before a dispute breaks out. (Prov. 17:14)
>
> Pride only breeds quarrels,
> but wisdom is found in those who take advice. (Prov. 13:10)
>
> A gentle answer turns away wrath,
> but a harsh word stirs up anger. (Prov. 15:1)
>
> Better a dry crust with peace and quiet
> than a house full of feasting, with strife. (Prov. 17:1)

Several other passages speak specifically of a "quarrelsome wife," but some husbands can be described that way, also. Both husbands and wives should avoid quarrels:

> Better to live on a corner of the roof
> than share a house with a quarrelsome wife. (Prov. 21:9; 25:24)

> A quarrelsome wife is like
> > a constant dripping on a rainy day;
> restraining her is like restraining the wind
> > or grasping oil with the hand. (Prov. 27:15–16)

The Bible is plain: Do not quarrel. Quarreling is foolish and is not appropriate in a loving home. Proverbs 14:1 tells us what happens when this is forgotten:

> The wise woman builds her house,
> > but with her own hands the foolish one tears hers down.

There is a reason that a wife is often called a "homemaker." In many cases, she is the one who sets the tone of the home. Will it be a warm, loving haven for the family? Will it be a hospitable home, one into which friends are welcome? Will it be a neat and tidy house? It is frequently the wife who makes the house a home, although the husband's role is just as important.

Yet no matter how neat the house is and how delicious the meals are, if the husband and wife continually quarrel with each other, if neither can ever do anything right in the other's eyes, the home will not be a pleasant place and the marriage will suffer. It is important to settle differences in a calm, kind way, without harsh arguments. Romans 12:18 says it best: "If it is possible, as far as it depends on you, live at peace with everyone." Of course, "everyone" includes your spouse and all your family, as well as outsiders.

There are two words that nearly "always" lead to quarrels and almost "never" should be used. So, avoid these words, especially when they are used in such statements as:

"You **always** spend too much money!"

"You **never** put your dirty socks in the laundry!"

These two words, "always" and "never," are usually exaggerations and are not helpful. They are often used in anger in the heat of an argument. Doing something two or three times does not make it "always," although that is often the reasoning behind angry criticism. Harsh statements by one make the other defensive and often lead to flaring tempers instead of good solutions.

It is much better to sit down and calmly discuss issues of difference without criticism. One can say, "When you spend too much money, it makes it difficult to have the money for what we really need." Or, "When you leave your dirty socks on the floor, it makes more work for me when I do the laundry." Find a loving way to let your spouse know when you are upset without exaggeration or criticism.

Rule #9
"'In your anger do not sin.' Do not let the sun go down while you are still angry, and do not give the devil a foothold" (Eph. 4:26–27).

It is good advice not to go to bed angry with each other. Settle problems as they arise, rather than letting them fester and become worse. The devil always tries to get us into situations in which we make the wrong choices. When you are angry, you are more vulnerable to his advances. So settle your differences while they are small and more easily reconciled. Always remember that you love each other and then treat each other with kindness and respect. Your marriage is more important than either of you individually.

Marriage, like a house, needs maintenance. If one neglects the small repairs that need to be made to the house, those repairs become major. In the same way, when there is a small problem in a marriage, if it is ignored, it may become a major problem. If the problems do begin to escalate, seek help before it is too late. It is usually not wise to discuss your problems with friends. It is better to seek someone who has had training in counseling and will keep your problems confidential. Go to a wise and respected elder of your congregation, or to a professional Christian counselor, but get the help you need.

In God's divine plan, divorce is not an option: "Therefore what God has joined together, let man not separate" (Matt. 19:6b; compare 1 Cor.

7:10 and Mal. 2:16). Although Moses allowed divorce under certain conditions (Deut. 24:1–4), Jesus said, "But it was not this way from the beginning" (Matt. 19:8b). In order to follow God's divine plan, we should work hard to make our marriage relationships the best possible. Managing our anger will help tremendously.

Rule #10
"Honor the Lord with your wealth" (Prov. 3:9).

Use whatever money is available to you in service to the Lord, because whatever you have really belongs to the Lord. When you are careless with money, it is the Lord's money you are wasting. You should set aside money for your contribution to the church before you spend for anything else. One should not be selfish and claim what he or she has as "mine!" The finances should be "ours," not "mine" or "yours."

It is wise to plan a budget to help you live within your means. Do not spend more than you make. Form the habit of saving money every payday, even if it is only a very small amount, and be consistent. Be sure to save that money, even if doing so means you must lower your standard of living. It is more important to spend less than you make than to "keep up with the Joneses." Make careful choices. Buy only what you really need, and resist impulse buying. Plan your spending carefully. Teach your children to handle their money wisely.

Rely on God, not on money. Remember that the love of money is the root of all kinds of evil (1 Tim. 6:10). Or as Proverbs says:

> Whoever trusts in his riches will fall. (Prov. 11:28b)

and

> Better a little with the fear of the Lord
> than great wealth with turmoil. (Prov. 15:16)

and

> Do not wear yourself out to get rich;
> have the wisdom to show restraint.

Cast but a glance at riches, and they are gone,
> for they will surely sprout wings
> and fly off to the sky like an eagle. (Prov. 23:4–5)

Do not want too much, and do not spend so much time working that there is no time to enjoy what you have.

Rule #11

"Therefore each of you must put off falsehood and speak truthfully to his neighbor, for we are all members of one body" (Eph. 4:25).

We all are called to be truthful with each other. If we should be honest with our fellow Christians, how much more should we be honest with our spouses!

Deception tears down relationships. Husbands and wives should cultivate the atmosphere of mutual trust and reliability. Each one should strive to be trustworthy in everything. There is no place in a loving relationship for deception of any kind. A good marriage is based on mutual trust, and that trust is dependent on open honesty and truthfulness. Keeping secrets from each other is usually foolish. It denies one's spouse the joy and comfort of trusting and being trusted. When secrets come between husband and wife, it will be difficult to trust each other.

Rule #12

*"May your fountain be blessed,
and may you rejoice in the wife of your youth.
A loving doe, a graceful deer—
may her breasts satisfy you always,
may you ever be captivated by her love" (Prov. 3:9).*

My father's advice to married couples was always, "Never stop courting each other." He took his own advice by continuing to court Mother until her death. They loved each other with *agape* love. Each of them put the other first in their plans. Each considered the other's viewpoint. They had a beautiful relationship that others recognized as being special. That realization came because they never stopped courting each other.

You can have this kind of relationship, too. Think back to the time when you met your spouse and you began to be interested in each other. You probably spent a lot of time trying to get his or her attention in order to show your interest. You probably put a lot of energy, thought, and planning into pleasing him or her. Courting paid off then and it will now. Never stop trying to please each other; never stop courting.[1]

Cultivate meaningful rituals—good-bye kisses, hugs, etc. Do whatever you can to show your love to your partner. Be protective of each other. Enjoy each other's company. As the years pass, your love for each other should grow deeper and more meaningful. The early excitement of physical love may diminish over time, but the deeper, more mature love will surpass the fledgling love of the early marriage.

As 1 Thessalonians 3:12a says, "May the Lord make your love increase and overflow for each other." This verse is addressed to all Christians. However, it is applicable to the marriage relationship as well as to the larger family of God.

Rule #13

*"A happy heart makes the face cheerful,
but heartache crushes the spirit" (Prov. 15:13).*

Stay friends. Make each other laugh. Enjoy each other's company. Do fun things together. Do not be afraid to have your own silly, private secrets and games. If you are going to have a midlife crisis, plan it together. Have fun with it. Share the excitement of doing new things together.

Share private jokes together. Share the book you are reading. Share whatever interests you. Share whatever interests your spouse. Share little loving rituals—a kiss as you pass in the hallway, a hug in the kitchen, watching the beauties of a sunset or a full moon. Enjoy each other. After all, you enjoyed each other while you were courting, and then you got married because you wanted to spend the rest of your lives together. Enjoy your marriage.

Rule #14
"Be imitators of God" (Eph. 5:1).

Both husbands and wives should strive to be as God-like as possible. Proverbs 31:10–31 is a very familiar passage about worthy women. First Timothy 3 and Titus 1 both describe the qualities that all Christian men should try to attain. Galatians 5:22–26 lists the fruit of the Spirit that all Christians need. Many other passages tell us how to live in Christ, according to God's will. Following the teachings of these passages will help us in our relationships, especially between husbands and wives.

Beatitudes for Married Couples

Someone has written "Beatitudes for Married Couples," and these were published anonymously in the bulletin of the Central Church of Christ (Houston, Texas), November 30, 1972:

1. Blessed are the husband and wife who continue to be affectionate, considerate, and loving after the wedding bells have ceased ringing.
2. Blessed are the husband and wife who are as polite and courteous to one another as they are to their friends.
3. Blessed are they who have a sense of humor, for this attribute will be a handy shock absorber.
4. Blessed are the married couples who abstain from alcoholic beverages.
5. Blessed are they who love their mates more than any other person in the world, and who joyfully fulfill their marriage vow of a lifetime of fidelity and mutual helpfulness to each other.

6. Blessed are they who remember to thank God for their food before they partake of it, and who set aside some time each day for reading of the Bible and prayer.
7. Blessed are they who attain parenthood, for children are a heritage of the Lord.
8. Blessed are those mates who never speak loudly to each other, and who make their home a place "where seldom is heard a discouraging word."
9. Blessed are the husband and wife who can work out their problems of adjustment without interference from relatives.
10. Blessed are the husband and wife who faithfully attend the worship of the church for the advancement of Christ's Kingdom.
11. Blessed is the couple who have complete understanding about financial matters, and who have worked out perfect partnership with all money under control of both.
12. Blessed are the husband and wife who humbly dedicate their loved ones and their home to Christ, and practice the teachings of Christ in their home, by being unselfish, loyal, and loving.

Correcting a Myth

J. Allan Petersen writes,

> Most people get married believing a myth—that marriage is a beautiful box full of all the things they have longed for: companionship, sexual fulfillment, intimacy, friendship....
>
> The truth is that marriage, at the start, is an empty box. You must put something in before you can take anything out. There is no love in marriage; love is in people, and people put it into marriage. There is no romance in marriage; people have to infuse it into their marriages.
>
> A couple must learn the art and form the habit of giving, loving, serving, praising—keeping the box full. If you take out more than you put in, the box will get empty.[2]

If you forget everything else that you have read in this chapter, at least remember two scriptures: "Give honor to marriage, and remain faithful to one another in marriage" (Heb. 13:4 NLT) and "[E]ach one of you also must love his wife as he loves himself, and the wife must respect her husband" (Eph. 5:33 NIV).

These two chapters on marriage are not intended to be comprehensive, but to provide some food for thought. I hope you will be drawn closer to each other as you are drawn closer to God by following his plans, and that you may thus make your marriage more meaningful.

My prayer for you is the same as the one Paul prayed for the Philippians:

> And this is my prayer: that your love may abound more and more in knowledge and depth of insight, so that you may be able to discern what is best and may be pure and blameless until the day of Christ, filled with the fruit of righteousness that comes through Jesus Christ—to the glory and praise of God. (Phil. 1:9–11)

―――――――FOR FURTHER THOUGHT―――――――

1. When you and your spouse were courting, what are some of the special things that you did for each other? Are you still doing any of those things? Why or why not?

2. Which of the scriptures cited in this chapter are most meaningful to you in your marriage? Why?

3. What scriptures can you think of that are not mentioned in this chapter that will help you have better relationships with others, especially with your spouse?

4. What is important to you in marriage? Make a list, and revise it as you give more thought to what is important to you.

5. What is at least one thing you are not currently doing that you can begin to do to enrich your relationship with your spouse?

6. What difference would it make in the way you spend your time together if the Lord were physically present with you?

Chapter Seven

Love Your Children

"Train the younger women to love their... children."
—Titus 2:4

God has given commands concerning our children. One command is that the older women should train the younger women to love their children (Titus 2:4). As we have seen in earlier chapters, we show our love for the Lord by obeying him. Thus as we follow God's plan to love our children, we show our love both for God and for our children. This perspective goes beyond normal human love for one's children.

Rearing children is one of the most important (and sometimes one of the most difficult and frustrating) things that humans do. It can also be one of the most rewarding. So, how would you like to have three "surefire, never-fail rules" for rearing your children?

All right, I admit it. I have exaggerated. I also realize that it is presumptuous to give rules for rearing children, but I am going to do it anyway, now that I have your attention. As a mother of three wonderful Christian children, and grandmother of six even more wonderful grandchildren, I may have earned the right to make a few suggestions. I am certainly among the "older women" of Titus 2:4. Although I cannot tell you how to train your children in every situation, perhaps I can help you to find some important principles that will guide you through the maze of child-rearing.

If you are going to make a cake, you do not just start putting in a little of this and a little of that, using whatever happens to fall into the mixing bowl, hoping it will turn out to be a good cake. Instead, you first decide what kind of cake you want and then select the proper recipe and follow it. You select the right ingredients, including them in the correct balance. The cake will turn out right only if you have a good plan and then follow it.

In the same way, you must have a good plan for how you want your children to turn out and then follow that plan. You and your spouse should decide what is important to you. Sit down together and write specific goals for what you want your children to learn. If you are a single parent, then your job is even more difficult, but it is just as important, perhaps even more so. Expecting your children to be "perfect" is not an option. They will not be perfect children and you will not be perfect parents. List realistic goals and write down ideas about how you intend to attain those goals. Revise your list as your children enter new stages of development. Keep the list current.

Perhaps the following rules will be of some value to you. These are things that I have learned through the years, rules that I must admit that I did not always follow. However, with many prayers, our children turned out well in spite of the imperfections of their parents.

There are three very important rules that will help you in rearing your children. These rules are simple to state and easily remembered. However, they are much more difficult to put into practice. Stated simply, the rules are: 1. Love your children, 2. Tell your children that you love them, and 3. Make your children feel loved.

We will discuss each of these, but you will have to decide for yourself the best way to deal with your own children, keeping in mind these three rules.

Rule #1
Love Your Children

You may think, "Of course I love my children! It's only natural! I don't have to be told to do that!" However, God has said: "Teach the older women to

... train the younger women to love their husbands and children" (Titus 2:3-4). Not only do these verses say that mothers need to be taught to love their children, but they also tell me that I, as an older woman, have a responsibility to do some of that teaching.

When God gives the command to "love your enemies" (Matt. 5:44), the Greek word, *agapao* is used. You will remember that this word relates to how we act more than how we feel: we act in a loving manner whether we feel like it or not. Although our actions can be commanded, feelings of what we usually call "love" probably cannot be commanded, although those feelings will be influenced by our actions.

When God says to train women to love their children, a form of *phileo* is used. This word for love refers to the fondness that one has for those in close relationships, including those within the family. Thus loving our children, having a fondness for them, can and should be learned.

We need to have both kinds of love for our children.

No matter how much you love your children, there is always room for improvement. God wants you to learn to love those precious gifts from him even more than you do now. But how can you learn to love, to have tender feelings for your children? One way is to recognize that they are gifts from God and a blessing to you:

> Sons are a heritage from the Lord,
> children a reward from him.
> Like arrows in the hands of a warrior
>   are sons born in one's youth.
>   Blessed is the man
>   whose quiver is full of them. (Ps. 127:3-4)

Attitudes toward our children are important. When we think of our children as blessings from God, it is easier to have tender feelings toward them. Other verses in the Old Testament also teach that children are a gift from God (see for examples, Gen. 17:16; 30:6; 33:5; Ruth 4:13; and Prov. 17:6).

Another way to learn to love your children is to enjoy them at every stage of their development. Have the attitude that whatever your child's age, it is the best and most enjoyable age. Much frustration in parenting is avoided when the characteristics of children at each particular age are understood, accepted, and appreciated. It can be exciting to see them grow and develop. One day they cannot do something, and the next, they can.

There will be times when you are extra tired and your children are extra fussy. Just remember: it will not always be that way. Keep reminding yourself how much you really do love your children. Take time to rest and to cuddle the fussy child, and you will both feel better.

A friend related to me a conversation that she had with her mother-in-law, who had reared three sons. "How did you always manage to treat those rambunctious boys so lovingly?" asked my friend.

The reply was, "Oh, it was easy. When they came into the house, I just pretended that they were the neighbor's kids!"

We tend to treat outsiders with more courtesy and respect than family members. But remember, *agape* love is a conscious choice, not a passing feeling; it determines how you treat your children. Acting in a loving way toward your children helps to bring out those tender feelings of *phileo* love. The following suggestions may help.

Follow the Golden Rule

Love your children enough to respect them and treat them with kindness and courtesy. The Golden Rule, "Do to others as you would have them do to you" (Luke 6:31), applies to your treatment of children as well as adults. Treat your children tenderly, not harshly. Remember that they have feelings that can be easily hurt and spirits that are easily crushed. As Ephesians 6:4 says, "Fathers, do not exasperate your children, instead, bring them up in the training and instruction of the Lord."

Be patient with them, realizing they will not always live up to your expectations. Be realistic, not expecting more than they are capable of doing. They will make mistakes, and so will you. Teach forgiveness by forgiving them and by asking for their forgiveness when you make mistakes. (Which you will!) Love them enough to try to understand their points of view. This involves listening to what they think, rather than telling them what you want their opinions to be.

Teach Them to Know God

Love your children enough to teach them to know God. Deuteronomy 6:6–9 emphasizes the importance of teaching God's commands to your children:

> These commandments that I give you today are to be upon your hearts. Impress them on your children. Talk about them when you sit at home and when you walk along the road, when you lie down and when you get up. Tie them as symbols on your hands and bind them on your foreheads. Write them on the doorframes of your houses and on your gates. (Deut. 6:6–9; see also Deut. 11:19–20; 31:12–13; Ps. 34:11; and Joel 1:3)

I have a friend who took that last statement literally. She has written Scripture verses on the frames of every door in her house. She has beautiful handwriting, so the scriptures are decorative as well as meaningful. She and her family are surrounded by God's words.

There are many times and many ways in which we can teach God's word to our children. Our teaching should not be limited to bedtime stories or Bible classes on Sunday. We need to watch for those teachable moments that come more often than we may realize. One day, our then-four-year-old daughter was in the car with me. She said, "When I say my prayers tonight, there is something I want to tell God."

I explained to her that she did not need to wait until that night, but she could pray to God anytime, anywhere. She was excited as she responded, "You mean, I can talk to him right now? Right here in the car?"

I assured her that she could, and she immediately bowed her head and said her prayer, while a prayer of thanksgiving for the important lesson she had just learned went up from my heart.

Talk to your children about God when you sit at home, when you go along the road, when you lie down, and when you get up. Be sure that they know the mighty things that God has done; be sure they know that he is the creator of the universe and all that is in it. They will be taught other things in school and by their friends, so be sure you tell them the truth about God before others give your child the wrong information. Psalm 78 emphasizes the importance of teaching our children about God and his mighty works:

> I will open my mouth in parables,
> I will utter hidden things, things from of old—
> what we have heard and known,
> what our fathers have told us.
> We will not hide them from their children;
> we will tell the next generation
> the praiseworthy deeds of the Lord,
> his power, and the wonders he has done.
> He decreed statutes for Jacob
> and established the law in Israel,
> which he commanded our forefathers
> to teach their children,
> so the next generation would know them,
> even the children yet to be born,
> and they in turn would tell their children.
> Then they would put their trust in God
> and would not forget his deeds
> but would keep his commands. (Ps. 78:2–7)

Teach Them Right from Wrong

There are commands to children in the Bible, such as Ephesians 6:1–3. But how will they know about them unless we tell them? Timothy's mother and grandmother taught him Scripture from the time he was very young (2 Tim. 1:5; 3:15). Moses's father-in-law gave him some advice concerning the Israelites. Jethro said, "Teach them the decrees and laws, and show them the way to live and the duties they are to perform" (Exod. 18:20).

That same advice is valuable in training our children. It is important that we teach them the difference between right and wrong, and that we find God's ordained standards of behavior in the Bible. We must teach our children these moral standards while they are little so they will grow up knowing how to act.

Read or tell Bible stories to your children frequently—during the day as well as at bedtime. This may require that you spend more time in studying the Bible yourself, but that is a good thing. Teach them Bible stories, but even more importantly, teach them to know God, to love him, to trust in him, and to put him first in their lives. Help them to see his glory and majesty and to be awed by his mighty works. Lead them to heaven. This is the most important thing we can do for our children.

Set an Example

Love your children enough to set the example of integrity, devotion to God, and righteousness, even if it means making changes in yourself. You cannot lead them to heaven unless you are traveling the road yourself.

Have family devotional times with your children. Let them hear your prayers, especially when you are praying for them. Let them see you studying your Bible. Have Bible storybooks available on the children's level. Sing with them. Teach them the names of the books of the Bible. Teach them memory verses, and remember to learn those verses yourself. Children are more likely to learn verses if they see that you are learning them, too.

If you want your children to be polite, you must be polite to them. If you want them to listen carefully to you, you must listen to them. If you want your children to speak kindly, you must speak kindly. Children are great imitators. With that in mind, if there is language you do not want your children to use, you must not use that language. Think of areas in which you need to change your behavior in order to be a good example for your children, and let them see your efforts at improvement.

Meet with Fellow Christians

Love your children enough to make whatever effort is necessary to take them to church and Bible class at every opportunity. Take them; do not just send them. Make attending the assemblies of the church a priority for you and your whole family. The earliest Christians recognized the importance of being with their brothers and sisters in Christ, so they met daily (Acts 2:42–47). Be sure your children grow up with the attitude that attendance at church assemblies is important. If they see that attendance is important to you, it will become important to them.

The gathering of the church is one of the main places where we, as well as our children, learn about God and the Bible. It is where our children will learn to worship with the family of God. It is also where our children will build relationships with fellow believers that will sustain them all their lives. It is important for them to learn early to worship the Lord God. The spiritual encouragement that we receive from meeting with fellow Christians to worship the Lord gives us strength for the rest of the week. The spiritual food we receive when we worship together in the assembly of the church is even more important than physical food. Hebrews 10:25 tells us, "Let us not give up meeting together, as some are in the habit of doing, but let us encourage one another."

Train Early

Love your children enough to start training them *early*. In one story,

> After a lecture by the late Francis Wayland Parker, great Chicago educator, a woman asked:
>
>> "How early can I begin the education of my child?"
>> "When will your child be born?"
>> "Born?" she gasped. "Why, he is already five years old!"
>> "My goodness, woman," he cried, "don't stand here talking to me—hurry home; already you have lost the best five years."[1]

Think of Jochebed and Amram with their son, Moses (Exod. 2:1–10; Num. 26:59). They had only a very few years until he was weaned to teach him enough about God to sustain him all those years when he was growing up in Pharaoh's household. He would learn nothing about God from Pharaoh's daughter. It was only from his own parents, in the first few years of his life, that he would learn about the one true living God, whom he was to serve as a mighty leader of God's people.

An important verse to impress upon our children is Ecclesiastes 12:1: "Remember your Creator in the days of your youth." Start early; do not wait until they are older to teach them about God. Establish the pattern of discussion and study while they are young. If you begin teaching them very early, you will be better at it by the time the questions they ask become more difficult to answer. If they see that you study the Bible, they will realize that doing so is important.

It is never too early to introduce them to the truths of God's word. Read to them even before they can understand. You never know how much they comprehend. They will learn little by little as you continue to repeat what they need to know. That is the way God teaches us: "He tells us everything over and over again, a line at a time, in very simple words" (Isa. 28:10 NLT).

Discipline Your Children

Love your children enough to discipline them. Discipline is mainly training rather than punishment, and such teaching is important:

> Train a child in the way he should go,
> and when he is old he will not turn from it. (Prov. 22:6)

However, sometimes it is necessary for discipline to include punishment, but never harsh or abusive punishment:

> The rod of correction imparts wisdom,
> but a child left to himself disgraces his mother. (Prov. 29:15)

and

> He who spares the rod hates his son,
> but he who loves him is careful to discipline him. (Prov. 13:24)

The story of Eli and his sons is found in 1 Samuel 2 and 3. Eli knew what evil things his sons were doing, but he did not restrain them, he did not discipline them, and God punished him. The sons were also punished, but it was Eli's responsibility to train them in God's way. Just so, it is the responsibility of parents today to train their children in proper behavior. It is important for both parents to be in agreement and to be consistent about discipline.

When you must punish, be sure to do it in love and not in anger. The punishment should never be harsh, but should be appropriate for the age of the child and for the severity of the disobedience. It should be something that will help the child to remember not to repeat the bad behavior. If you merely send your misbehaving children to their rooms, they may not know why. They may feel isolated, rejected, and rebellious unless you explain to them exactly what the punishment is for and what you expect of them. Do not make them feel rejected. Make it a learning experience. Teach them how to overcome their problems, whatever they are.

It is important to discipline our children, to teach them, from the time they are very young. It is easier to teach a toddler than a teenager how to handle anger (and other bad habits). The best time to teach children anything is right now. It will never become any easier. They are learning something now—either what you want to teach them, or something else. If they are learning the wrong things, then later those wrong things will have to be un-learned and the right things taught instead. It is easier on both you and your children to teach them right behavior from the beginning.

> Discipline your son, and he will give you peace;
> he will bring delight to your soul. (Prov. 29:17)

The goal of discipline should always be to teach the child to discipline himself. Telling your children, "As long as you are in MY house, you will follow MY rules!" is not the best way to train them. It is much better to explain the reasons for the rules and the benefits of following them. Your children will grow up and leave your house. Will they then think that they have the right to do all the things you would not let them do, or will they have learned to do what is right? It is up to you to teach them self-discipline.

It is important that you set limits for your children. How else will they learn to set them for themselves? There will probably be times when your children will be glad you said "no" to something their friends want them to do. That way they can say, "My parents won't let me." That statement is easier for the friends to accept than the child saying, "I don't want to." At other times, they may not like the limits you set, but they will thank you in years to come when they look back and see that you were right.

Teach Them to Be Responsible

Love your children enough to teach them to accept responsibility for their own actions. This is a difficult thing to teach. Sometimes it is harder on the parents than on the children. Allowing them to avoid the consequences of their actions by always bailing them out of self-inflicted trouble is not loving them.

Saul is an example of one who had not learned to accept responsibility for his own actions. In 1 Samuel 15, we see that he did not obey God's commands to destroy completely the enemies of God, the Amalekites. Yet he claimed that he had obeyed God. When Samuel confronted him with the truth, Saul tried to place the blame on his soldiers. Samuel had to confront him again with the truth before Saul admitted his sin. This episode led to the kingdom being taken away from Saul. Eve is another one who did not accept responsibility for her own actions but tried to place the blame on someone else, and Adam did the same thing (Genesis 3).

Our children must learn to accept responsibility for their actions in order to become mature, competent, godly adults. Children learn by imitation, thus as parents we should model responsibility in all areas of our lives—work, friendships, church, and family. Our children are not fooled when we tell them one thing and then do another. We must be responsible for our actions before we can teach our children responsibility. Talk with them about some of the things you have done and are doing to be a responsible parent. Let them learn from the way you handle various situations.

One way of teaching responsibility is to make contracts with your children. Sit down when everyone is calm to discuss a problem that the children have—perhaps a messy bedroom or a tendency to forget to take out the trash. Be sure the children know why it is important for them to do what you insist must be done or why they should act in a certain way. If they think they really should not have to do whatever it is, listen carefully to their side of the story. Perhaps you are asking too much, or perhaps they do not understand what is expected of them.

Discuss the problem with them and make a compromise agreeable both to the parents and to the children. Be sure that they know it is the parents who are in charge and who make the rules. However, it is important for the children to know that they will be heard. They have the right to express their side of the problem. They need to know that you will listen to their viewpoint.

Let the children suggest what they think the consequences should be if they do not live up to their part of the contract. They will probably suggest something more severe than you would. Decide together what all of you think would be fair. If necessary, write in time limits, an inspection schedule, or anything else that would be helpful and agreeable to all. Put it in writing and have both parties sign it.

The purpose of this is to put the burden of responsibility on the children, so do not nag. Even if you think they are not going to make the deadline according to the contract, keep quiet! Wait quietly and calmly until the time limit is up, and follow the contract exactly. If they did not do what they agreed to do, let them suffer the already agreed-upon consequences. It is their fault if they did not live up to their promise, not yours.

But it is your responsibility to enforce the terms of the contract. Give them loving support and renew the contract. Next time, they will be more likely to fulfill the conditions of the contract. You will be helping your children to accept responsibility.

Do not try to tackle everything in one contract. Keep it simple. Emphasize the one thing you are trying to correct. Then later work on another problem in the same way.

Accepting responsibility for one's actions is closely related to making good decisions.

Teach Them to Make Good Decisions

Love your children enough to teach them how to make good decisions, starting when they are very young. As they are learning to make age-appropriate choices, they will make some bad ones, but they will learn from that. They must make decisions, even bad ones, in order to learn how to make good ones. The consequences of a third grader learning to think for himself are not nearly so serious as for an eighteen year old who has not learned to make wise choices. Be supportive, give them guidance, but let them make appropriate decisions for themselves, and then let them live with the consequences of those decisions. If the parents always bail the children out of unpleasant situations caused by bad decisions, then the children will not learn the valuable lesson of cause-and-effect. They will not learn to care for themselves. Sometimes they must suffer the consequences in order to learn that lesson. However, do not put a burden of too many decisions, or decisions that are too difficult, on them.

Do not let them make decisions that may put them in danger. For example, do not allow them to decide whether or not they will fasten the seat belts in the car. You, the parent, must still make the important rules and decisions.

Assign chores to your children, and then encourage them to make the decision to follow through and do those chores consistently. This is how they learn to pull their share of the load. Even toddlers can be given simple tasks, such as helping to pick up toys and put them away. Being part of the family means doing part of the work that is necessary for the functioning of the family. Learning to work cheerfully in the family is also good training for their jobs when they are grown. Learning a good work ethic early is very important.

Pay Attention to Your Children
Love your children enough to *listen* to them. It is important to pay attention even to babies. The children most likely to be obedient are those whose parents listened to them attentively and responded quickly while they were still babies.

When you are listening to your children, make eye contact with them—that way they know you are really listening. Give them your undivided attention when they are talking to you. If you listen courteously to your children, they will learn to listen to you.

Spend Time with Your Children
Love your children enough to spend time with them. The importance of this can be illustrated by a young couple falling in love. No one needs to tell them that they ought to spend time together. As their love develops, they will naturally want to be together as much as possible. In the same way, parents should spend time with their children in order to develop the love between them and their children.

It is also important to teach your children to love each other. If Johnny is frequently reminded that his little sister follows him around because she loves him so much that she wants to be with him, he will learn something about love. Instead of thinking of her as a pest, he will be complimented that she loves him. And *maybe* he will even try to act in a way to be worthy of that love.

Teach Them to Be Pleasant
Love your children enough to teach them to be lovable as well as loving.

That is, help them learn how to be pleasant and polite around other people, and how not to be offensive, hateful, or rude. This is the best way to get other people to treat your children the way you want them to be treated.

Teach your children to use good manners, not just in polite company, but in the family as well. Help them to overcome bad habits, such as interrupting when someone else is talking, or whining to get their way. Allowing your children to become brats is not loving them, nor is it teaching them to love others. It also makes it difficult for others to love them or even to see them as lovable.

Protect Your Children

Love your children enough to protect them. We put our babies in car seats and make the older children wear seat belts. We insist that our children look carefully both ways before crossing the street. Those are ways to protect them from physical harm.

It is even more important to protect them from spiritual harm. That may mean not allowing them to go to certain events that their friends attend, or to watch certain TV shows. We need to be discerning about our entertainment and teach our children to be discerning, also. If we want to protect our children from evil, we will not allow them to attend unwholesome movies or watch such programs on television. It is important to teach our children why they should not take part in such activities. Teach them to be selective. Be strong enough to withstand their pleading. Learn to say no. Doing so may make them angry, but eventually, they will recognize and respect the fact that you had the courage, strength, maturity, and wisdom to stand firm.

There may be a movie or TV program that the older children really want to see, but you are not convinced that it is all right. In that case, it may be helpful for you to watch it with them. If you see that it really is something they should not see, you can turn it off, and if it is not that bad, then you can help them to evaluate what they are seeing and hearing. Let it be a learning experience as you discuss what is wrong and why. Do not just tell them what is wrong, but ask them what they think. Guide them into understanding why what they are seeing is bad. Doing so will teach them how to think for themselves. They will learn how to protect themselves from bad influences. It will also help you to know your children better and to bond with them on a deeper level. It will show them that they matter to you and that you are willing to listen to them.

One mother, who has taught her children to be selective by watching what they watch and then talking with them about what they had seen, told me, "Our kids say it's okay if TV or internet filters aren't always reliable since we've installed 'kid filters' in each of our children that are very effective. These filters are difficult to install and can require frequent maintenance and upgrades. Once in place, however, they are extremely reliable." God protects us, his children, from spiritual harm by giving us his armor to fend off the attacks of the devil (Eph. 6:10–18). In the same way, we must provide our children with whatever they need to withstand Satan's temptations. We must also teach them to avoid situations that may lead to trouble.

Teach them God's word so that they can remain true to that word. Help them learn to live a pure life.

Pray

Love your children enough to pray for them, and for yourself. You need God's help to rear your children to be the God-fearing adults that he wants them to be. One important way to show your children that you love them is to let them hear you mention them by name in prayer to God. Doing this lets the children see how important they are to you and to God. Let them hear you thank God for them and for all the good things he is helping them to do. If they have not been listening to your prayer, they will when they hear their own names.

The Bible gives us the example of David praying for his son Solomon: "And give my son Solomon the wholehearted devotion to keep your commands, requirements and decrees and to do everything to build the palatial structure for which I have provided" (1 Chron. 29:19). We should follow David's example in this and pray often about our children. Our prayers should be specific. Pray, "Help Mary as she studies for her math test tomorrow. May she be able to remember the things that she studies." That is better than merely saying, "Bless Mary." Hearing you pray for specific things for them will help motivate your children to do what you have prayed for God to help them do. At the same time, you will be teaching them how to pray.

Teach Them to Be Independent

Love your children enough to teach them to be independent. One of your main jobs as a parent is to work yourself out of a job. You will not be around all their lives to do things for them, so they must learn to take care of themselves. Parents spoil their children when they do for them what the children can and should do for themselves.

Help Them Develop Their Talents

Love your children enough to help them develop their talents. They may have abilities that are artistic, musical, academic, athletic, or something else. Encourage them to realize their potential. Give them opportunities to follow their interests so that they can learn what they are capable of doing. It has been said that, "Children are not things to be molded, but are people to be unfolded."[2]

One of the most important ways of showing your love for your family is through prayer. When Hannah brought Samuel to Eli, she said, "As surely as you live, my lord, I am the woman who stood here beside you praying to the Lord. I prayed for this child, and the Lord has granted me what I asked of him. So now I give him to the Lord. For his whole life he will be given over to the Lord" (1 Sam. 1:26–28). May you pray for your children as Hannah did for Samuel, and may your children serve the Lord their whole lives.

---FOR FURTHER THOUGHT---

1. How can you teach your children to know God?

2. Read Proverbs 25:28. In what ways do you see the truth of this, either in your own life or the lives of your children?

3. How can you help your children learn self-control or self-discipline? Think of specific examples of what has worked for you.

4. What are some ways your parents helped you learn to be responsible? How does Luke 16:10–12. apply to teaching children responsibility?

Chapter Eight

Make Your Children Feel Loved

"Train a child in the way he should go."
—Proverbs 22:6

The suggestions in this chapter and the previous one are not exhaustive, but I hope they will be helpful. You will be able to find other ways of developing and showing your love for your children. Be creative in finding what works for you and your family.

In chapter seven, we considered Rule Number 1: Love Your Children. Now we go to:

Rule #2
Tell Your Children That You Love Them

Actions may speak louder than words, but words are still very important. We do many things because we love our children, but the children probably do not realize that is why we do these things. We provide homes for them, we prepare food for them, we make sure that they have clothing, we care for them when they are sick. We do all this because we love them. But how do they know unless we tell them? Of course, we do not say it in a way that will make them feel guilty. We want to encourage them by the way we tell them.

God is our father, and he does many things for us because he loves us. But if we did not have his word in John 3:16 (and other passages), we might not realize that he sent his son because he loves us so much. In the same way, we need to tell our children of our love for them. They will not know unless we tell them.

Jesus set an example when he stated his love for us in John 15:9: "As the Father has loved me, so have I loved you." He not only showed us his love, but he also declared it verbally. In the same way, we need to tell our children that we love them.

There are many benefits to saying "I love you" out loud. It improves the atmosphere of the home by making those who hear it feel good. When we feel good, we naturally act better. Saying these words lays a foundation for a discussion of other important matters of the heart. Hearing these words makes it easier for the children to accept the corrections we must give them. We give many verbal instructions and corrections, and all should be done in the context of love. Verbalizing our love helps to balance out the other things our children hear from us. It puts our discipline in the proper context. The children learn that we insist on their proper behavior because we love them, not because we want to make life difficult for them.

Some people find it difficult to say these words, but if we cannot speak freely this central truth of our relationships, how can we hope to discuss appropriately other important but difficult matters?

Different Ways to Say "I Love You"

Remind your children daily of how much they mean to you. Show them by your actions that you love them, but also say it to them. Do not let a day pass without saying "I love you" to each child—and then think of other meaningful ways of stating your love. For example:

"I am so glad you are my child!"
"I missed you while you were gone today. I'm glad you are back home."
"I really like it when you give me such sweet hugs and kisses."
"Thank you for helping me today; I'm proud of the way you worked."
"I'm glad God made you a part of our family."

When children are not told that they are loved, they may have difficulty expressing their love for others even in later life. The lack of that love may adversely affect their own marriages. If children do not receive the love they need as children, they are more likely to look for that love in the wrong places as adults. A friend who is the father of a teenager said recently, "I hug my daughter a lot, because I know that if I don't, some other guy will!"

Mothers are often considered to be more nurturing than fathers, but the father's role is also critically important, especially with daughters. All children need to have a strong father figure in their lives, and both parents are responsible for nurturing each of their children. Both boys and girls need to receive love from each parent. The younger they are when they start receiving this love, the better.

When our granddaughter was a toddler, sometimes when she was playing and her daddy was watching her, he would sternly call her name. Startled, she would look up at him quickly, and he would smile at her and softly say, "I love you." And she would beam all over. Not only was he stating his love for her, but he was training her to listen to him. When she heard his voice, she did not know if he was correcting her behavior or telling her of his love. She quickly learned to listen any time he spoke to her.

Too often the only time parents talk to their children is when they are correcting them, telling them what to do, or scolding them. There will be times when you must address such issues, but do it lovingly. Negative comments, especially when given harshly, can hurt deeply. Be positive in your comments to your children. Remember the old saying, "You can catch more flies with honey than you can with vinegar."

Notice the good things your children do and compliment them. Let them know that you notice and appreciate them. You probably brag on your children to other people, so why not brag on them to the children themselves? They need to hear you saying good things to them as well as about them. They will appreciate it more than you know. And they will try harder to please you.

Another way that your children can hear of your love is to pray with them and ask God to bless them. Let them hear their names often in your prayers.

Touch Your Children

Touch is an important way of helping you to say, "I love you." It is much easier to say those words while holding your child close. Even Jesus touched the children as he told them of his love by blessing them: "And he took the children in his arms, put his hands on them and blessed them" (Mark 10:16).

Some children who are not caressed enough may even go to the extreme of misbehaving so badly that they know they will be spanked. At least then they are being touched and are receiving attention from their parents. This desire to be touched is often called "skin hunger."

Hugs and kisses, although extremely important, are not the only ways of showing affection. Think of other ways to express your love. For instance, a back rub at bedtime is one way to satisfy the need for physical contact as well as to relax the child and prepare for sleep. This could also be a good time to talk over the events of the day and to verbalize your love. When children are relaxed and comfortable, they are more likely to open up and talk to you about their inner feelings. This time of talking with your children is important in telling them that you love them.

Each child is different and must be treated differently. Find the best way to tell each child of your love, and repeat it often every day. It is very important to say "I love you" to your children frequently. In fact, the words they hear you say to them most often should be "I love you!"

So, Rule #1 is Love Your Children, and Rule #2 is Tell Your Children That You Love Them. But Rule #3 is probably the most difficult to implement as well as the most crucial rule of all.

RULE #3

Make Your Children Feel Loved

Children who feel secure in their parents' love are less likely to be rebellious. The child who thinks, "They don't love me! If they did they would let me go to that R-rated movie with my friends!" is more likely to misbehave and be a problem.

Notice that I did not say your children will never rebel if you love them enough. (Remember Adam and Eve?) Instead, I said that they are less likely to rebel if they know they are loved. When they feel loved, they know that you want what is best for them in the long run, and they are more willing to accept your restrictions.

But how can you make your children know and feel that they are loved? That is the difficult part. As I have said, each child is different. You must observe your own children to see what works with each of them. However, a few suggestions may help you understand how to use this rule.

Laugh Together

Laughter can help to keep the lines of communication open. If there is already a problem, laughing together can help re-establish communication. Look for jokes, and be aware of funny things that happen around you. Cultivate private family jokes. But remember: laugh *with* them, never *at* them. Laughing at your children will crush their spirits. Proverbs 17:22 speaks to the importance of laughing with and not at them:

> A cheerful heart is good medicine,
> but a crushed spirit dries up the bones.

Be sure that your children know that you enjoy them. Spend time with each child. Play, talk, laugh, work together. Do whatever the child wants to do while developing a spirit of family togetherness. Tell your children and tell others that you love and enjoy your children. Make whatever age they happen to be the most enjoyable age of all.

Encourage Family Traditions

It is especially at holiday times that traditions are expected and enjoyed. Birthday celebrations can be full of traditions. When our children were small, one tradition was that each child was allowed to plan the menu for the birthday dinner. One daughter always chose barbecued chicken; our son always chose pecan pie instead of birthday cake. Those choices were traditional. Some families have elaborate birthday parties, while others celebrate quietly with only the family. Certain games may always be played at certain times. Anything that the children expect to be done can become a tradition. Make it fun and something they look forward to doing.

One year, I made a Christmas tree ornament for each of the children and grandchildren. I did the same thing the next year, and now, over twenty years later, we all still enjoy that tradition. So make up your own traditions—whatever is fun for you and your family.

Establish Routines

Any routine will need to be flexible, certainly not rigid; but predictability is important for a child's feeling of security. It helps to know what to expect. A consistent bedtime routine is especially important to children. That routine should certainly include Bible stories and prayers.

Establish early the routine of having the children do age-appropriate chores. Doing their chores consistently fosters responsibility as well as a sense of belonging in the family.

Another routine that is important is eating meals together. That is a good time to discuss the day's happenings. It is a good time to communicate with each other and learn what is going on in the lives of your children. It is also a good time for a family devotional and a discussion of God's word. Make meal time a positive and pleasant family time. It is a time to learn and to become closer together, not a time to criticize or grumble.

Preparing the meals together can also be time well spent. Teach your children, both boys and girls, how to cook. Make learning fun. They likely will be more willing to try new foods if they have helped prepare them.

Establish whatever routines will make things better for your family. Perhaps having a family fun night once a week would be good. It could be a time for playing games together or doing special things the children like to do. It could be a time to do special service projects for other people. It is important for a family to spend time together on a regular basis.

Build Memories

Surely you have childhood memories that you cherish, so what memories do you want your children to cherish? One woman told me that what she remembers most are the things her family always did (kept traditions) and the times that they did something totally outside the routine (broke traditions).

What are you doing, or can you do, to build happy memories? One way is to do fun things together. However, be sure it is something the children think is fun, not just what you like to do!

One young mother wrote the following tribute to her father:

> **Father's Day Memories**
> A long time ago, when I was the age my children are now, I used to have the most wonderful tea parties with my Daddy. He had to sit on the floor because he's so tall, but he was a most delightful guest. (Years later, Mother told me how terribly bored he had been. But he loved me enough to endure. When asked about it now, he only smiles!) When I was a little older, my Dad (a college professor) taught a class on church history at our congregation. I was thrilled to be able to attend and studied (and struggled) hard to keep up. I wanted so very much to enter the world of this man who was always such a special part of my world. Although there was no way I (barely a teenager) could then grasp most of the (college level) material covered in that class, somehow Dad convinced me both that it was worthwhile to continue trying, and that it was all right if I didn't understand everything. Today, I am still grateful to be blessed with such a father.[1]

If you do not supply good memories, your children will remember only bad times. They have only one childhood in which to build those memories, so do not miss out on opportunities. Expose them to as many different wholesome activities as possible. Become interested in what interests them. Be involved in their activities without smothering them.

Wonder with them at the beauties of God's creation. Small children are fascinated with all manner of bugs. When your children are watching bugs crawl on the sidewalk, watch with them. Teach them about nature. Watch a beautiful sunset with them. Look at the stars on a clear night and teach your children that God created these beautiful things for us to enjoy. Feel the awe and wonder that your children feel as they discover the marvels of God's creation all around them.

Most of all, be sure that they will remember the times you taught them from the Bible, the times that they learned about the one true, living, Almighty God. These are the memories that will sustain them all their lives.

Be a Home-maker

Create a warm home atmosphere—a haven. If at all possible, one parent should be there when children come home after school. Coming into an empty house gives a child an empty feeling. If you have ever been disappointed when you expected someone to be there to greet you, you can relate in a small way to how the child feels.

When your children come home, greet them warmly and positively. That is not the time to nag them about something they have done or not done. Wait until after they have told you about their day and perhaps have had a snack. Make them glad to be back home with you. Then gently correct them; never nag them.

Include your children, when possible and appropriate, in making plans that involve the whole family. Let the children express their thoughts about vacation plans and meal menus, for instance.

Home should be a happy place, a safe place. Children feel loved when they know there is some place they can go where they are protected from the outside world. Bad things may happen to them, but when they come home, it is important for them to know that the love of their parents will surround them and protect them. As loving parents, we will provide that comforting atmosphere for them, even as our loving father in heaven provides protection and comfort for us.

Be Positive

When giving instructions to your children, if possible tell them, "Do this," instead of "Don't do that." For example, saying, "Please hang your jacket in the closet" is better than saying, "Don't drop your jacket on that chair!"

When you tell a child, "Don't jump on the bed," the last thing the child hears is "Jump on the bed!" So he does. It would be more meaningful to say, "When you are on the bed, lie down." Then the last thing heard is "Lie down." Let the phrase that you want obeyed be the one that echoes in their minds.

Never let your children hear you criticize or belittle them to other people. That hurts. Instead, let them overhear you telling a friend what wonderful children you have. Surely you can find something really good about them to tell someone else, especially when the children think you do not know they are listening. However, be especially careful not to tell their "cute, but naughty" actions in front of them: that will encourage more mischief!

Help your children to feel good about themselves. Praise them whenever you can, but avoid vague "Good girl/boy" statements. If you tell your child, "You have really been good today; I'm proud of you," be sure the child really has been good all day. You may not know something the child has done that was naughty, but the child may think you do know, and that you are pleased with it! It is better to focus on something good that you know the child has done, and praise him/her for that. Be specific with praise and focus on actions and attitudes.

When your children accomplish something worthwhile, compliment them and encourage them to continue. However, remember that false praise is counterproductive. Praise their efforts, not just the outcome.

When they fail at something, let them know that you still love them, and help them to do better next time. Always be there for your children. Be available to listen to them and to help them, but do not do everything for them. Allow and encourage them to do what they can for themselves.

Although there is no such thing as too much love, there is a danger of doting and spoiling, neither of which is love. Doting is giving your children everything they want because they are just so cute you cannot resist. Spoiling is doing for children what they can and should do for themselves.

It is important to give much attention and love to your children, but if your home becomes overly child-centered, there will be neither happy parents nor happy children. You must not allow the children to be in charge. That is a burden too heavy for them to bear. Children must still obey their parents (Col. 3:20).

Take Care of Yourself

We have been talking about love that wants what is best for the child's own good, with no selfishness involved. However, you cannot sacrifice yourself totally for your children. One of the best things you can do for your children is to keep yourself spiritually healthy. So do what you must, and take some time for yourself to rest, to study, and to pray.

I have a friend who has made it a routine to take one hour each morning in which the children cannot disturb her. They know that this is her quiet time to spend alone with God. They know that after that hour she will devote time to them, but she has taught them that her time with God each day is extremely important, and they respect that. They, too, spend some of that time in similar activities. They have a list of things they can do while their mother is studying, praying, and meditating on God's word. Of course, part of their list is the same as what she is doing. When they were babies, her time with God was spent while nursing the baby, or maybe just holding him close. As the children grew older, they might color a picture about a Bible story that they had read together from a children's Bible. Then she would help them to add the picture to a timeline that they made together. As they matured, their list continued to be age appropriate. Now that they are teenagers, they need less direction in observing the quiet hour with God for themselves. She and her husband have taught their children the importance of spending time alone with God every day.

If your children see you as valuable and deserving of care and respect, they will feel all the more special when you give them attention. If they see you as a doormat, nothing you do for them will be enough to fill their needs.

Another important thing you can do for your children as well as for yourself is to keep the husband/wife relationship as God would have it to be. The best thing a father can do for his children is to love their mother; and the best thing a mother can do for her children is to love their father. Be sure that your children see that you love each other. Children feel more secure in a home where love is evident. If you are a single parent, then you have an even more difficult job in creating this loving home atmosphere alone, but with God's help it can be done. Perhaps you have family members who can assist you. Or your brothers and sisters in Christ should be able to help you. In that way, they would be following God's command to love one another (1 John 4:11, and others).

Do Not Show Favoritism

I recall reading an article years ago about a woman who knew she did not have long to live and wanted to leave a special message for each of her children. She wrote a letter to each one to be delivered after her death. In each letter, she told the child, "You don't have to tell the others, but you were always my favorite." Then she went on to tell special things about each child. The children cherished the letters and felt loved by their mother. It was years later when they finally compared their letters and realized what she had done.

It is all right if each of your children believes that he or she is your favorite and accepts the responsibility of being especially kind to the others because of it. You must recognize that each child is different and will have different needs, but do not play favorites. This can be especially important if one child is chronically ill or has special needs or has serious behavioral problems. When one child must have special attention, parents must be careful not to let the other children feel neglected. Treat your children differently, but make sure that each child feels completely loved!

God's Example

God is our father, and he is a loving parent. He loves us, he tells us in his inspired Word that he loves us, and everything that he does for us should make us feel loved. Therefore we ought to follow his example as we deal with our own children. However, we are human, and we do not always respond to God's love the way we should. Look at Adam and Eve. Although they had the great privilege of walking in the garden with God, who loved them totally, they disobeyed him. So we should not be too surprised if our children, whom we love dearly, do not always respond according to our wishes.

Obviously, I cannot tell you exactly how to rear your own children, but I hope I have given you some helpful ideas that you can expand upon. I will close by repeating the three rules: Love your children. Tell your children that you love them. And make them feel loved.

My prayer for you is that you will pray, pray, pray, pray, pray. As you are dealing with the challenges of rearing your children according to God's will, you will need his help. But you may not know how to ask for it; you may not know how to pray or what to pray for. Do not worry about that. Just pray, because "[T]he Spirit helps us in our weakness. We do not know what we ought to pray for, but the Spirit himself intercedes for us with groans that words cannot express. And he who searches our hearts knows the mind of the Spirit, because the Spirit intercedes for the saints in accordance with God's will" (Rom. 8:26–27).

---FOR FURTHER THOUGHT---

1. What do you think is especially important for your children to learn? How can these things be taught?

2. How can you make your children feel more loved?

3. What are some rules of etiquette that you want your children to learn? Why are these important, and how can you teach them?

4. As you think about this chapter, how would you organize it? Would you move some of the suggestions to other rules? Which ones would you move, and why? What other suggestions would you add?

CHAPTER NINE

LOVE ONE ANOTHER

"Since God so loved us, we also ought to love one another."
—1 JOHN 4:11

In the first chapter of this book, we explored the meaning of *agape* love and discussed two of the three parts of its definition: how God shows his love to us, and how we show our love to God. The emphasis in this chapter is on the third part of that definition: how we show love to others, especially to our brothers and sisters in Christ.

A NEW COMMAND

"A new command I give you: Love one another. As I have loved you, so you must love one another. By this all men will know that you are my disciples, if you love one another" (John 13:34–35). In a casual reading, this statement by Jesus may not seem to be a *new* command. After all, even as far back as the Old Testament, God's people were told to "Love your neighbor as yourself" (Lev. 19:18b). However, Milton Jones has pointed out three areas in which this command is new:[1]

> 1. THE OBJECT. In Leviticus, the object of the love that God commands is one's neighbor. In Jesus's teaching, the object is broadened to include not only all of one's fellow disciples but also one's enemies (Matt. 5:44). Nevertheless, there is a special love for fellow believers. If we spend our energy loving those outside the church but neglect to show proper love to those in the church, then problems and splits will

develop within the body of Christ. And that should not be. We need to be especially loving toward fellow Christians in order to preserve the unity that God wants for us.

2. THE MEASURE. In Leviticus, the measure of love is one's self. Love your neighbor to the same extent that you love yourself. In Jesus's statement, the command is elevated to the level of his love for us. He loved us enough to lay down his life for us. This teaching and example constitute a new definition of love. And he wants us to love other Christians to that same extent. Christ's love for us is the measure of love that we should have for our brothers and sisters in Christ.

3. THE PURPOSE. In Leviticus, the purpose is to obey God: "I am the Lord. Keep my decrees" (19:18b–19a). In Jesus's statement, the purpose is that others may identify his disciples. We should have such deep love for our fellow Christians that outsiders will see the difference in our lives and know that we are truly disciples of the Lord. That observation should make them want to know more about the Lord and his church. It should make them want to be a part of such a loving community. The purpose of loving one another is not only to obey God but also to bring others to Christ. Thus the purpose of this new command is to be evangelistic.

The object of love, the measure of love, and the purpose of love are all new in this "new command" that Jesus gave his disciples. And that new command applies to all his disciples, including us today.

Love One Another

The instructions the Lord gave about how we should treat our fellow Christians are quite clear. Many times, Jesus told his disciples to love one another, and the word he used was *agape*. At least twenty of the "one another" passages in the New Testament make reference to loving one another.[2] So it is obvious that loving our brothers and sisters in Christ is a direct command of God, one that we must not ignore.

The goal of loving our fellow Christians is our soul's salvation. We cannot enter heaven except for the love of God, both God's love for us and our love for God. We cannot love God unless we love our fellow Christians: "For anyone who does not love his brother, whom he has seen, cannot love God, whom he has not seen. And he has given us this command: Whoever loves God must also love his brother" (1 John 4:20b-21).

We usually think that the opposite of love is hate. However, the opposite is really indifference. Love says, "I care about you and I will act toward you the same as Jesus does." Indifference says, "I don't care anything about you, because you are worth nothing to me."

We have seen that *agape* love involves how we treat others—it is action more than emotion. Therefore, loving our brothers and sisters in Christ means that we will treat them in a loving way, with kindness, consideration, and respect, putting them ahead of ourselves, without any selfishness.

Live a Life of Love

Our philosophy of life should be to live a life of love according to God's will (Eph.5:2). In Romans 12:1, we are told to offer our bodies as living sacrifices—that is, to live the totality of our lives in worship to God. The rest of that chapter tells us how to act:

> Love must be sincere. Hate what is evil; cling to what is good. Be devoted to one another in brotherly love. Honor one another above yourselves. Never be lacking in zeal, but keep your spiritual fervor, serving the Lord. Be joyful in hope, patient in affliction, faithful in prayer. Share with God's people who are in need. Practice hospitality. (Rom.12:9-13)

Hospitality is not just opening your home to visitors and serving them a nice meal. It also sincerely promotes goodness and love of others. It puts others interests above one's own. It includes the spiritual side in serving the Lord joyfully, patiently, and faithfully. It is not limited to family and friends, but includes those from whom we expect nothing in return. It provides for the needy. All of this is part of hospitality. Romans 12 continues:

> Bless those who persecute you; bless and do not curse. Rejoice with those who rejoice; mourn with those who mourn. Live in harmony with one another. Do not be proud, but be willing to associate with people of low position. Do not be conceited. (Rom.12:14–16)

The Lord said to love our enemies. Blessing those who persecute us or curse us is one way to show that love. We need to learn the best way to interact with those around us. Are they happy? Be happy with them. Are they sad? Be sad with them. Do not be so proud of yourself that you ignore or mistreat others.

> Do not repay anyone evil for evil. Be careful to do what is right in the eyes of everybody. If it is possible, as far as it depends on you, live at peace with everyone. Do not take revenge, my friends, but leave room for God's wrath, for it is written: "It is mine to avenge; I will repay," says the Lord. On the contrary:
>
> > "If your enemy is hungry, feed him;
> > If he is thirsty, give him something to drink.
> > In doing this, you will heap burning coals on his head."
>
> Do not be overcome by evil, but overcome evil with good. (Rom. 12:17–21)

The things mentioned in the rest of Romans 12 have to do with being at peace with others. Taking revenge only escalates the warfare. Besides, God is the one who will avenge all wrongs. We must do good to our enemies and let God judge if they should be punished. He will do what is needed.

Love Fulfills the Law

Romans 13 relates love to fulfillment of the law of Moses:

> Let no debt remain outstanding, except the continuing debt to love one another, for he who loves his fellowman has fulfilled the law. The commandments, "Do not commit adultery," "Do not murder," "Do not steal," "Do not covet," and whatever other commandment there may be, are summed up in this one rule: "Love

your neighbor as yourself." Love does no harm to its neighbor. Therefore love is the fulfillment of the law. (Rom. 13:8–10)

Jesus told his disciples that he came to fulfill the law, not to abolish it (Matt. 5:17). He accomplished this by living a perfect, sinless life of love. His love for us was demonstrated by his coming to earth and dying to take away our sins (1 John 4:9–11). Everything he did was done out of love for us. Although we can never live such a perfect life, we should strive to imitate his life of love (Eph. 5:1–2). Our motivation for loving others should be that he first loved us (1 John 4:19). We should try to love others in the same way, and to the same extent, that he loved us.

The Lord's love for us is not dependent on whether or not we love him. Our love for him (or lack of that love) does not motivate him to love us more or less. On the contrary, he continues to love us even when we do not show any love for him and in spite of the many sins that we commit. What a blessing his love is to us!

The Apostle of Love

When John was young, Jesus called him a "Son of Thunder" (Mark 3:17). Yet in his old age, he was known as the "Apostle of Love."[3] The only thing that will fully account for this growth and maturity is his association with Jesus, learning about love from the master teacher. John spent his life maturing in the same kind of love that Jesus showers daily on all his followers. That same transforming love will change our lives (Titus 3:3–7).

John gives us important insights into that love in 1 John. He assures us that God has lavished his love upon us by allowing us to become his children (1 John 3:1). Therefore it is up to us to behave properly as his children: "This is how we know who the children of God are and who the children of the devil are: Anyone who does not do what is right is not a child of God; nor is anyone who does not love his brother" (1 John 3:10). Cain did not love his brother—in fact, he murdered him (1 John 3:12). In the Sermon on the Mount, Jesus redefined murder: "You have heard that it was said to the people long ago, 'Do not murder, and anyone who murders will be subject to judgment.' But I tell you that anyone who is angry with his brother will be subject to judgment" (Matt. 5:21-22). This new definition is made even plainer in 1 John 3:15: "Anyone who hates his brother is a murderer, and you know that no murderer has eternal life in him."

If we truly love our brothers and sisters in Christ, we will not have that kind of anger against them; we will not hate them, nor will we ignore them. John goes on to say that we should have the same kind of love for our fellow Christians that Jesus had when he died for us (1 John 3:16-20). And we show that love by the way we act toward others—the way we take care of those in need. It is not enough to express our love verbally—we must act on that love: "Dear children, let us not love with words or tongue but with actions and in truth" (1 John 3:18).

1 John 4:7-12 teaches several important lessons about love: Love comes from God. Those who love know God. God is love. God showed his love by sending his son as an atoning sacrifice so that we might live. Love is not that we loved God, but that God loved us. Because God loved us, we ought to love others. If we love, God lives in us. His love is made complete in us.

1 John 4:16-21 continues with these important lessons: We can rely on God's love. When we live in love, we live in God. Love is complete so that we shall have no fear at the judgment. We love because he first loved us. We cannot love God and hate our brothers and sisters. If we do not love those we can see, we cannot love God, whom we cannot see. It is a command of God that "Whoever loves God must also love his brother" (1 John 4:21).

Chapter 5 of 1 John teaches us still more about love: "[E]veryone who loves the father loves his child as well. This is how we know that we love the children of God by loving God and carrying out his commands. This is love for God: to obey his commands" (1 John 5:1b-3).

Our love for God is shown by our obedience. Thus we see the importance of obeying God in all his commands, and especially the command to love one another. However, God has given us other commands concerning how we act toward our fellow Christians and we should obey those commands as well. We shall see what those commands are as we consider more of the "one another" passages.

Live in Peace with One Another

God's commands teach us how to treat fellow Christians. Mark 9:50b tells us "to be at peace with each other." Romans 14:19 tells us to "Make every effort to do what leads to peace and to mutual edification." Romans 12:16 adds, "Live in harmony with one another." Jesus says something similar in John 6:43: "Stop grumbling among yourselves." And James 5:9 says, "Don't grumble against each other, brothers."

Also in the Old Testament, the Lord was concerned that his people should live peacefully and in unity. Psalm 133:1 is an example:

> "How good and pleasant it is
> when brothers live together in unity!"

Feuding and fighting have no place among the Lord's servants. We should all strive to be peace-makers.

Encourage One Another

It is easier to encourage one another when living in peace. In Romans 1:12, Paul wrote, "[T]hat you and I may be mutually encouraged by each other's faith." After telling the Thessalonians about the second coming of the Lord, he tells them in 1 Thessalonians 4:18 to "encourage each other with these words." And in 5:11, he says much the same thing: "Therefore encourage one another and build each other up." Hebrews 10:24 is similar: "[L]et us consider how we may spur one another on toward love and good deeds."

If we act in a loving manner toward others, it will be easier to encourage them. To act lovingly means that we pay attention to others and become aware of their needs so that we can help and encourage them. It is discouraging to be slighted or ignored.

Have a Spirit of Unity with One Another

Encouraging one another will build a spirit of unity. Romans 15:5–6 tells us: "May the God who gives endurance and encouragement give you a spirit of unity among yourselves as you follow Christ Jesus, so that with one heart and mouth you may glorify the God and Father of our Lord Jesus Christ." According to Romans 12:5, we belong to each other in unity: "So in Christ we who are many form one body, and each member belongs to all the others." God wants unity, not division among his followers: "So that there should be no division in the body, but that its parts should have equal concern for each other" (1 Cor. 12:25).

Acceptance of each other is important to God and thus should be to us: "Accept one another, then, just as Christ accepted you in order to bring praise to God" (Rom. 15:7). If we are united, we will "Carry each other's burdens" (Gal. 6:2; see also Eph. 4:2 and Col. 3:13). As members of one body, we will also "speak truthfully" (Eph. 4:25) to each other.

Serve One Another

In John 13:14–15, Jesus told his disciples, "Now that I, your Lord and Teacher, have washed your feet, you also should wash one another's feet. I have set you an example that you should do as I have done for you." We should serve others as humbly as Jesus served his disciples. Galatians 5:13 also commands us to be servants: "[S]erve one another in love."

Serving involves doing good deeds, good actions, or good works. We do these things not in order to be saved, but rather we do them out of love and gratitude because we have been saved. As Christians we should be involved in doing good things. That is what God prepared us to do. Ephesians 2:8–10 assures us of this:

> For it is by grace you have been saved, through faith—and this not from yourselves, it is the gift of God—not by works, so that

no one can boast. For we are God's workmanship, created in Christ Jesus to do good works, which God prepared in advance for us to do.

Thus we see that we have been created by God to do good. One purpose of doing good deeds is to glorify God. "In the same way, let your light shine before men, that they may see your good deeds and praise your Father in heaven" (Matt. 5:16). In other words, we do not serve others in order to boast about what we have done or to make ourselves look good in the eyes of others. We do them because we want others to know that we are children of God. We want to tell others what God has done for us. We want them to know that our good deeds have been done through God (John 3:21). We want God to be glorified.

Good Deeds

What are some of the "good works" that Christians should do? Sometimes we wish for a checklist telling us exactly what to do and how to do it. Although the Bible may not contain the kind of lists that we would desire, it does mention some things that we can do. We have already referred to Romans 12. A shorter list is in Luke 6:27–31: "Love your enemies, do good to those who hate you, bless those who curse you, pray for those who mistreat you.... Do unto others as you would have them do to you."

Another work God requires of us is that we believe in Jesus and the one who sent him (John 6:28–29). This faith requires more than mental assent. We must trust him enough to live in obedience to his commands (Matt. 19:16–17).

Romans 12:13 tells us to practice hospitality. Verse 15 tells us to rejoice with those who are happy and mourn with those who are sad. That is, we must care enough about others to know what they need and then supply that need.

First Corinthians 10:24 tells us to seek the good of others instead of ourselves; that is, we must not be selfish. As Paul discusses the characteristics of love in 1 Corinthians 13, he shows us that selfishness has no place in godly love. We should consider what we can do for others, and then do what is good for them.

First Timothy 6:17–18 commands the rich to be rich in good deeds.

An important passage is 2 Timothy 3:16–17: "All Scripture is God-breathed and is useful for teaching, rebuking, correcting and training in righteousness, so that the man of God may be thoroughly equipped for every good work." We need to study the Bible in order to be ready to do the good works that God's grace enables us to do (2 Cor. 9:8).

James 4:17 tells us the result of not doing good deeds: "Anyone, then, who knows the good he ought to do and doesn't do it, sins."

Hebrews 6:10 assures us that "God is not unjust; he will not forget your works and the love you have shown him as you have helped his people and continue to help them." Remember, when you do good to God's people, you are doing good to God himself. One way of showing love to God is to act lovingly toward his disciples (compare Matt. 25:40).

Galatians 6:9–10 encourages us to persevere in doing good: "Let us not become weary in doing good, for at the proper time we will reap a harvest if we do not give up. Therefore, as we have opportunity, let us do good to all people, especially to those who belong to the family of believers."

Love Is Forever

In addition to the verses that tell us to "love one another," we also have Paul's great treatise on love in 1 Corinthians 13. This is one of the best-known and most beloved chapters in the Bible. Paul wrote it to tell the Corinthians how to handle the problems they were having in the church—how to treat those who belong to the family of believers. The Corinthians were having problems that were splitting the church. For one thing, those who had the gift of speaking in tongues seemed to think that their gift made them superior to those who did not have that gift. Rather than condemning them for that attitude, Paul took a more positive route. He showed them that not only were their gifts temporary, but there is something much better that is permanent: love. If they treated fellow Christians with godly love, they would not have the attitude of superiority that was detrimental to the unity of the Lord's church.

Although Paul did not write this chapter to be read at modern weddings, it is appropriate in that setting. Husbands and wives should treat each other with the same *agape* love that dictates how we treat our fellow Christians. This *agape* love will transform our lives.

How Do We Show Our Love to Others?

The love described in 1 Corinthians 13 is the *agape* love that we should have for one another. These characteristics also reveal God's love for us, because God himself is love (1 John 4:8, 16). Thus, while Paul was describing the way love acts, he was also describing the way God acts. Therefore, if we want to imitate God (Eph. 5:1), we must work to embody the description in 1 Corinthians 13.

We can do nothing to deserve the love of God, but he freely gives it to us anyway. That is one of the blessings that he showers upon us daily. His love never fails. Because of that great love, we should respond to it gratefully. And how we respond is important, especially as we relate to our fellow Christians.

First Corinthians 13 defines love in ways that deserve close attention. It is a beautiful description of love. It tells the members of the church at Corinth that they should act lovingly toward the other members in imitation of God's love for them. Paul's words, written by the inspiration of God, are just as important to us today as they were to the original audience.[4]

As we look more closely at 1 Corinthians 13 in chapter ten of this book, my prayer is that it will lead all of us into an even more loving relationship with all our fellow Christians. No matter how loving our relationships are in the church, there is always room for improvement, as Paul wrote to the Thessalonians: "Now about brotherly love we do not need to write to you, for you yourselves have been taught by God to love each other. And in fact, you do love all the brothers throughout Macedonia. Yet we urge you, brothers, to do so more and more" (1 Thess. 4:9–10).

---FOR FURTHER THOUGHT---

1. In what ways is John 13:34–35 a *new* command? Explain.

2. What does it mean to "live a life of love" (Eph. 5:2)?

3. In Matthew 5:17, Jesus told his disciples that he came to fulfill the law, not to abolish it. How did he accomplish this?

4. What are some of the important lessons about love that are found in 1 John? Which of these lessons do you think that you need the most?

5. There are a number of "one another" passages in the New Testament. Which ones mean the most to you? Why?

CHAPTER TEN

LOVE, THE MOST EXCELLENT WAY

"And now I will show you the most excellent way."
—1 CORINTHIANS 12:31B

It has been said that love is the most powerful force in the universe. Love is so important in the lives of Christians that Paul says he is nothing without it (1 Cor. 13:2). In the same way, without love, we are nothing. So let us explore in more detail that powerful force that we need so desperately in our lives every day.[1]

Remember, *agape* love is action more than emotion. The words used to describe love in 1 Corinthians 13:4–7 are mostly adjectives in many English translations, but in Greek they are all verbs. This reinforces the fact that love is active, not merely descriptive. No matter how one feels, love demands action that will bring good to others. Godly love is unconditional goodwill, which demands victory over our selfish inclinations.

Again, because God is love, Paul's discussion of love gives us a glimpse into the mind and character of God. As we consider these characteristics of love, we should try to incorporate them into our daily lives.

First Corinthians 13 can be divided into three parts. Verses 1–3 discuss the supremacy of love; verses 4–7 consider the characteristics of love; and verses 8–13 tell of the permanence of love. Our main emphasis here is the characteristics of love.

Love Is Patient

The Bible says that without love, we are nothing. The Bible also says that love is patient. So, if we do not have patience, then neither do we have love and, therefore, we are nothing. Just what kind of patience does Paul mean?

Have you ever been impatient because your computer was slow to come on and you had to wait to get started on your project? Or maybe you were stalled in heavy traffic when you were late for an appointment? Or did the plumbing overflow just before your special company arrived? These problems may cause you to feel impatient; however, Paul is not concerned about patience with things or events. His emphasis is on being patient with people, especially our brothers and sisters in Christ.

Sometimes we see a new, immature Christian doing something that we know is wrong. We may be tempted to lose patience and think, "She ought to know better than that! I knew she wasn't going to be a very good Christian anyway. Just look at the kind of life she has lived!" But that is the very person with whom we need to have the most patience. Instead of criticizing her, probably behind her back, we need to show love to her by helping her to see her sin and then leading her lovingly and gently back to right behavior. This kind of behavior on our part is taught in Galatians 6:1: "Dear brothers and sisters, if another Christian is overcome by some sin, you who are godly should gently and humbly help that person back onto the right path" (NLT).

We must have patience with our brothers and sisters who are learning to walk God's way just as we have patience with toddlers who are learning to walk. When my grandson takes a tumble, you're not going to catch ME saying, "I knew he couldn't walk right! He might as well quit trying and save us all a lot of trouble!" No matter how many times he falls down, I will do what any of you would: I will stretch out my hands and say, "Oops! Here I am; let me help you!" We should have that same kind of patience when fellow Christians stumble. We should be quick to help them back up and set them on the right way again.

God is always there to pick us up when we stumble—no matter how many times we fall. God is patient (2 Pet. 3:9), and his patience is infinite. The call to love is an invitation to be like God; thus, we should endeavor to have the same kind of patience with others that God has with us.

Love Is Kind

Kindness can be defined as goodness in action. This goodness includes thinking of the needs of another person and doing what we can to show sympathy and goodwill. It includes helping that person in whatever way we can. It is being considerate and gentle. Kindness leaves no room for harshness in dealings with others. Kindness demands that one be tender and compassionate, showing sympathy and caring. Kindness is an integral part of the nature of God (Rom. 2:4). It is how he treats us. His kindness toward us involves grace and mercy. Our salvation is made possible only through the kindness, grace, and mercy of God.

This sort of godly kindness is not part of our natural human inclinations. We want others to be kind to us, but we want to take care of ourselves before we spend time on others. However, we cannot let selfishness keep us from being kind. We must make a conscious effort to make kindness a part of our lives.

However, we should not let "kindness" lead us to ignore what is wrong and should be corrected. It is not being kind nor loving to the sinner to ignore his sins and leave him in his lost state. As someone has said, "We must be careful of 'sloppy *agape*.'"

"Sloppy *agape*" says, "Oh, I love you too much to upset you by telling you that you are in sin." Real love says, "You are wrong, and I want to help you get it right."

Neither is it kind to our children to let them get by with unbecoming behavior because we do not want to make them, or ourselves, unhappy by disciplining them. True kindness teaches them to behave properly.

We cannot be guided by a vague, convictionless desire to make everything pleasant for another person. Love is not a doormat. True kindness must occasionally require what is unpleasant. Sometimes "tough love" is needed. Even then we must not forget to be kind when we confront a fellow Christian, because unkindness hurts and it wrecks lives. Unkindness hurts both the one who receives the unkindness and the one being unkind. Our unkindness to others often gives us a guilty conscience, and a guilty conscience always hurts.

Kindness, like the other aspects of love described by Paul in this chapter, should become a way of life for us, because we want to be like God as we learn more about him.

Love Is Not Jealous

The Bible tells us that love is not jealous, yet it also tells us that our God is a jealous God (Exod. 20:5; 34:14; Deut. 4:24). How can that seeming contradiction be? How can it be wrong to be jealous if God himself is jealous?

The *Greek-English Lexicon* by Dankers and Bauer, et al, gives these definitions of *zelos*: "1. intense positive interest in something" and "2. intense negative feelings over another's achievements or success."[2] So we see that the same Greek word, *zelos*, can be either positive or negative. It can be translated as "zeal," which is usually good, or "jealousy," which is usually bad. One must look at the context to decide what is meant.

Perhaps Galatians 4:17–18 will help to understand: "Those people are zealous to win you over, but for no good. What they want is to alienate you from us, so that you may be zealous for them. It is fine to be zealous, provided the purpose is good." These verses show both bad and good jealousy. "Those people" are the ones who are jealous of the attention being given to Paul, and they want all the attention for themselves—a bad jealousy.

A good purpose leads to good zeal. In 2 Corinthians 11:2–4, Paul says that he is jealous with a godly jealousy for the Corinthians. He is afraid that they are being deceived by someone with a different gospel.

Good jealousy, or zeal, is an intense emotion, embodying ardor and zealousness. It includes a belief that something rightly belongs to the one who is jealous. God knows that he is the almighty creator and Lord of the universe and that he rightly deserves praise and honor from us. It is for our own good that we should also recognize that fact. When we ignore God, turn away from him, and do not put him first in our lives, he intensely longs for us to return to him and worship him only. His godly jealousy wants us to do what is right. He wants us to accept the fact that honor, glory, and worship belong to him and him only. He wants this because he knows that it is for our own benefit that we worship him, and thus his jealousy is good.

Bad jealousy, or envy, is selfish. It is primarily interested in self and does not care about others. It begrudges the successes of others. It has an improper view of fairness: something is "fair" only if it benefits the jealous one instead of someone else. Ungodly jealousy makes unreasonable demands on the attention of others. Bad jealousy is often the motive for committing various sins. This is the jealousy that God condemns.

When we are jealous of someone else, it usually means that we are too concerned with ourselves. We want all the attention, we want all the interest of others, we want the best of everything for ourselves. But God's jealousy is different. He is not concerned with himself, but with us:

> God's jealousy is not the peevish, anxious, irritable, capricious thing that human jealousy is. God's jealousy means God calls man to turn his life toward God. That is what men need. Nowhere else can we find real love, happiness, or peace. Nowhere else can we find life. God's jealousy produces man's blessing. . . . God's jealousy is really God's love.[3]

God always wants for us what is best; therefore he calls us to turn our lives toward him and him alone.

If we have the same love for others that God has for us, we will not be jealous of others. If we are jealous of someone, then we must act lovingly toward that person. As we want what is best for him or her, our jealousy will be overcome by love.

Love Does Not Boast

No one likes to be around people who are always bragging about themselves and what they have done. A braggart soon becomes irritating and tiresome. Yet, we ourselves are too often eager for our chance to talk about what we have done.

There are many ways we are boastful, perhaps without even thinking about it. We try to "top" someone else's story. Or, we say things like:

> "I was right, I told you so!"
> "Well, at least I'm more humble than he is!"

Often unnecessary money is spent on material things just for bragging rights. Someone wants to have the fanciest car; someone else wants everyone to know how big and beautiful her house is.

We need to avoid boasting, but we also need to show compassion to those who are caught in this trap. I have known people who bragged that they were given preferential treatment by their doctor, by salespeople, by their friends, by nearly everyone. They left the impression that they thought, "I'm so good that I deserve special treatment from everyone, including you." My impression was that they actually felt inferior, and because of that they were trying to convince others that they were important enough to be loved and to be given special treatment. Anyone who acts this way needs our love, because a braggart, no matter how obnoxious, is crying out for help. And, as Christians, our job is to help those who have needs.

Name-dropping is a way of boasting that we know famous people. The Christians in ancient Corinth were active in name-dropping. One said, "Well, Paul is my leader!" Another claimed to follow Apollos, and still another Peter (1 Cor. 1:12). They thought their importance was dependent on their leader. And indeed, our importance does come from our leader, when our leader is Christ. What need is there for us to boast about anything on this earth when God has blessed us with "every spiritual blessing in Christ" (Eph. 1:3)? We cannot possibly find anything to boast about that is better than being "a chosen people, a royal priesthood, a holy nation, a people belonging to God" (1 Pet. 2:9).

No matter how much we brag, no human recognition will ever compare with the awesomeness of the recognition God has given us through Christ. We do not need to try to elevate ourselves before men. Christ set us free from the burden of boasting by showing us how truly important we are to the Creator and Ruler of the entire universe: "How great is the love the Father has lavished on us, that we should be called children of God! And that is what we are!" (1 John 3:1).

If we talk about what God has done for us in lavishing love on us, that is not boasting about anything we have done, it is praising God. It is God's grace that makes him care for us, not anything we have done. Love is not boastful because it recognizes and is thankful for God's grace as it works to transform each of us into a person of worth. (See also 2 Cor. 10:13-18 and Gal. 6:14)

It is difficult to love others when we think about ourselves too much. Boasting is based on preoccupation with self. A Christian, however, thinks first of God and then of others. Self-centeredness draws one inward and is grasping. Christian love reaches out, and is giving.

Love Is Not Arrogant

Tony Ash writes:

> I don't know how creampuffs are made. But it looks like someone took a biscuit, put some goo on top, pumped some air into the middle, and squirted some more goo into the hole. People can

be creampuffs, too. That's a person who is swollen up because he is pumped full of his own importance. He certainly couldn't care very much about me or about anyone else. How could he? He is too full of himself.

A puffed up personality reminds me of a Greek verb related to the word for a bellows. The verb indicates a person who has been inflated or caused to swell, as if by a bellows. Paul uses that verb to describe a particular unloving type of person. It is translated "puffed up," "giving himself airs," "cherishing an inflated idea of his importance," and "being conceited." The RSV translation says, "Love is not arrogant!"

The idea of someone being pumped up like a balloon suggests a comic figure who would go "whoosh" if punctured. But in a real life situation it's not funny.[4]

Perhaps you have heard about the fellow who was so arrogant that he strutted even while sitting down! A person who is arrogant is full of his own importance. If others do not recognize his importance, he is sure to call their attention to it. Perhaps he really is important, but if, in his arrogance, he flaunts it, others will be made uncomfortable. The opposite of arrogance is modesty. It is much more comfortable to be around someone who is modest about his accomplishments than to be with someone who is arrogant.

An arrogant person is more interested in himself than in anyone else. He may think that he is above the rules that others must follow. It is not uncommon to hear of such people in the nightly news. Arrogance leads one to think he or she already knows everything and does not need to continue studying God's word to find out his will. Thus an arrogant person appears to be a know-it-all. In discussing spiritual things with others, the arrogant person often is more interested in proving himself right than in learning the truth. Those who were arrogant in Corinth were probably making everyone else miserable, and that is not a loving way to treat fellow Christians. In the same way, if we are arrogant today, we will make others miserable.

When we find ourselves becoming arrogant, the first thing we should do is confess our fault to God and then ask him to help us overcome it. As with everything in our lives, we should try to imitate Jesus and the life of love that he lived and encouraged his disciples to live. Paul must have learned this lesson, for he wrote to the Philippians, "Do nothing out of selfish ambition or vain conceit, but in humility consider others better than yourselves" (Phil. 2:3). Peter offered similar advice: "Humble yourselves, therefore, under God's mighty hand, that he may lift you up in due time" (1 Pet. 5:6).

When love, *agape* love, controls our lives, there is no room for arrogance.

Love Is Not Rude

Although we should be polite to those we love, Paul is talking about a different kind of rudeness. It is not merely being impolite—forgetting to say "please" and "thank you." According to Danker's *Lexicon*, the Greek verb used here means to "behave disgracefully, dishonorably, indecently"; that is, behaving in an unseemly manner, or disgracing oneself.[5] It often refers to sexual indecency. It includes both what one does and how one feels. One can do something disgraceful and feel no shame, or one can feel the shame that results from disgraceful activities. The common idea here is "shame."

Today's New International Version of the Bible translates this phrase as love "does not dishonor others." The phrase could also be translated, "Love does not act in a shameful or indecent way." Love does not make indecent advances toward others. If I do something to shame or disgrace myself, that is my problem, but it has little to do with my love for others. Because 1 Corinthians 13 discusses relationships, verse 5 should be understood as it applies to the way I relate to others. Love does not dishonor, offend, or belittle others; it will not insult or humiliate; it will do nothing to shame another person. Instead, it respects, encourages, and builds up others.

We do not eliminate rudeness by keeping rules of etiquette but by showing love to others in imitation of our Lord. We should always be considerate of others and respect them. Common courtesy is important, but it is even more important to avoid shaming the people around us. Any rudeness that shames or disgraces a brother or sister puts stumbling blocks in that person's way. Any act that shows love to others will help pave the way to the kind of relationships that God wants for us.

Love Is Not Selfish

This part of verse 5 is translated in various ways: "it is not self-seeking" (NIV); "does not demand its own way" (NLT); and is "not selfish" (ERV); among others. A literal translation would be it "seeks not its own things" (that is, things pertaining to self).

Sometimes we are like the little boy who could not get his way with his playmates, so he took his ball and went home. Because he had the only ball, no one was able to play. Everyone, including the boy himself, was hurt by his selfishness. He avoided giving in to the wishes of the others, but what was the result? His selfishness ruined the fun for everyone.

There is a difference between selfishness and healthy self-interest. The Bible teaches us to love our neighbors as ourselves (Lev. 19:18; Luke 10:25–28). If we do not love ourselves, then neither can we love our neighbors. Therefore healthy self-love and self-interest must be part of God's plan for us. Putting too much emphasis on the self is wrong and causes problems, but one should never feel guilty for having proper self-love. Although we should put others first, we cannot neglect ourselves. Taking proper care of ourselves is not necessarily selfish.

The interest I have in myself has to be considered in terms of my relation to God and others. If I retreat from serving God and others and do only what pleases me, I limit myself to serving my own ego. And there is nothing in the universe smaller than a person who is all wrapped up in himself.

Have you noticed how many of the descriptions of love that we have discussed are in some way the antithesis of selfishness? Thinking too highly of oneself, or selfishness, is the basis of many other sins, but love is the remedy for selfishness. Just think how trouble-free and delightful our world would be if all selfishness could be eliminated and replaced with love!

I recall hearing a story many years ago illustrating the difference between heaven and hell. In hell, those who were there could not bend their elbows. They were all sitting at a table loaded with wonderful, delicious food. Yet they were miserable and starving because they could not bend their elbows to bring the delicious-smelling food to their mouths. Meanwhile, those in heaven were also unable to bend their elbows. They, too, were sitting at a table loaded with wonderful, delicious food. Yet they were all happy and well fed because each one was feeding the person sitting across the table. They did not need to bend their elbows when they unselfishly fed their neighbors.

If one is consumed with his own selfishness, it is impossible to put into practice the kind of love that is described in 1 Corinthians 13. However, unselfishness is related to all of the characteristics of love in this chapter.

Remember that you can have "JOY" by serving Jesus first, Others second, and Yourself third.

Love Is Not Irritable

In 1 Corinthians 13:5, Paul refers to the irritations that occur in human relationships. The word Paul uses here has to do with an explosion—an intense inner experience that moves one to action. Terrible consequences often follow an explosive irritation. We can think of the eruption of Mount

Vesuvius that destroyed Pompeii and Herculaneum. When we become angry and lose our tempers, our explosions can be just as destructive to relationships as that eruption was to the surrounding countryside. In an unguarded moment, any of us could say a word or commit an action that will take years to overcome. Self-centeredness makes us explode at others, and it is the opposite of the patience discussed earlier. A patient person is not easily provoked.

An intense inner experience that moves us to action is not necessarily bad. It could be something good, depending upon what irritates us and how we react to that irritation. For instance, Jesus was irritated enough to cleanse the temple by driving out those who were misusing it (Mark 11:15–17). He did not lose his temper and explode: he was righteously punishing those who deserved it.

We should not be "hot-tempered" or easily angered. Yet, despite our best efforts, we will fail, because none of us has yet achieved perfect love. God is still working on us and we must be willing subjects, even though we have flaws. We should pray that God will forgive us when we explode and then help us to develop such inner reserves that nothing will upset us to the point of explosion at a fellow Christian.

Love Is Not Resentful

Some translations say, "Love keeps no record of wrongs." The Greek word used here is a mathematical term that refers to entering something into a record book so that it can be remembered later. Thus this verse says that love does not enter evil done to it in a ledger to consider later.

We often continue to mull over things that should be forgotten. As we think again and again about some wrong done to us, we become resentful, and we want to get even! We *like* to get even! But think about it. What kind of world would we have if everyone spent their time getting even?

Jesus has turned our lives around. Thus Paul's reminder that "love is not resentful" relates to our commitment to our Lord. We may want to be resentful, but because of Jesus, we will drive those thoughts from our minds. Because of Jesus, God does not hold our sins against us—he does not enter them into some heavenly ledger to be used against us on the final day. Instead, he writes our names in the Lamb's book of life (Rev. 21:27). Because of Christ, God offers us reconciliation to himself (2 Cor. 5:18-21). He rejects the claims of vengeance. He does not want to "get even" with us when we sin. He wants to save us. Thus, he has wiped clean the record of debt of our sins (Col. 2:14).

If God does not dwell on wrongs done to him, neither should we dwell on wrongs that another person has done to us. Love does not keep score; it forgives and *forgets*. But it is almost impossible to forget those wrongs if we allow ourselves to think about them over and over. When those remembrances come to us, we must consciously make ourselves think about something else. Following the commands in Philippians 4:8-9 will help to control our thoughts.

Those who have been forgiven by God should also forgive others. And if we are to forgive, then we must drive resentment out of our lives, because resentment is caused by an unforgiving spirit.

Love Does Not Delight in Evil, but Rejoices in the Truth

Studying the Bible and learning the truths of God's Word brings joy to us. However, Paul has in mind how we react to others rather than how we react to what God has told us.

Perhaps you have had a part in persuading a sinner to put on Christ in baptism. If so, tears of joy may have streamed from your eyes. It is easy to rejoice in that person's decision to accept the truth.

On the other hand, love does *not* rejoice when a brother or sister in Christ embraces falsehood and turns from the truth. Wrong has no real joy in it. When I sin, I have no joy—I may think I am happy, but I have no real joy. Neither should I be joyful when someone else sins. In this passage,

Paul places his focus on the wrongs of others. Therefore, if I love someone, I do not rejoice when that other person sins. Because love deals with human relations, Paul means we should be glad when someone turns to God and tries to live according to his will, and never be glad when anyone stumbles and falls.

In a bad situation, love wants to help, but when the situation is good, love wants to celebrate with joy:

> Christianity is a joyful religion. Joy is at the very heart of it. God invented joy, and he intends to give it to his people. If they don't get it, they have missed much of what Christianity is about. After all, Jesus did not come to make us miserable. Gospel means good news, not bad news!
>
> Paul says, "Love does not rejoice in wrong, but rejoices in the right." This gets to the center of Christian joy. It isn't a superficial "rah-rah" thing. We don't manufacture it out of our emotions. It drinks deeply from the heart of God.[6]

Paul was in prison when he wrote the Philippians to "Rejoice in the Lord always. I will say it again: Rejoice!" (Phil. 4:4). We may wonder how he could say that when he was in chains. It was because he knew that God was with him and that he was doing God's will—he was in tune with the heart of God. At another time, he and Silas could sing songs of praise to God in the middle of the night even after having been severely beaten and chained in prison (Acts 16:22–25). Paul demonstrated the same kind of joy that Jesus had as he went to the Cross: "Let us fix our eyes on Jesus, the author and perfecter of our faith, who for the joy set before him endured the cross, scorning its shame, and sat down at the right hand of the throne of God" (Heb. 12:2). Godly joy is a deep-down feeling that comes from knowing and obeying God's truth, which we learn by studying the Bible.

There is a difference between knowing the truth and speaking the truth. Because Paul is concerned with relationships, being truthful with each other is of great importance. It is also a major concern in Ephesians 4:15, where Paul urges Christians to "speak the truth in love." A literal translation of the Greek would be "truthing in love," or "being truthful in love." Thus, it is not enough to speak the truth; our actions should be truthful, also.

Later in the same chapter, Paul writes, "Therefore each of you must put off falsehood and speak truthfully to his neighbor, for we are all members of one body" (Eph. 4:25). Some people may tell the truth when it is in their own best interests, but Christians have a better motive for being truthful: it is because we are members of the body of Christ.

Sometimes we may think that truth and love are opposed to each other. We may think that it would not be loving to speak the truth about a friend's sins. However, real love is loyal to truth. Real love will tell that friend to repent from sin and turn back to God. Truth and love are not in contrast, but go together. We will rejoice when that friend is back on the road to heaven.

Love Always Protects

According to Danker's *Lexicon*, the Greek word used here, *stergo*, frequently carries the sense of "covering or enclosing in such a way as to keep something undesirable from coming in, as water into a ship."[7] Thus this verse could be translated, "Love springs no leak." That is, love keeps confidences and does not leak information that should be kept private. It covers over and does not gossip about wrongs that others have done. Of course, there are times when the sin is public and should be dealt with publicly, but all too often information is repeated unnecessarily and hurtfully. That is not the way love acts. Love recognizes that exposure is not always the best method of bringing the sinner back to a right relationship with God. Love will protect the sinner from having sins exposed unnecessarily. Love does not gossip about the shortcomings and sins of others. Love will help the person overcome sin. Love's motive is to save the soul of the sinner.

Danker gives another meaning of *stergo* as "to bear up against difficulties, bear, stand, endure."[8] Some translations say, "Love bears all things."

That is, love hangs in there, even when it is difficult to continue. We may find a fellow Christian to be extremely unlovable, but that is the very person who most needs our loving attention and help. We must learn to love the sinner while hating the sin. And we must never confuse the two.

Lovingly protecting the reputation of other Christians is a key to avoiding many difficulties of relationships in the church.

Love Always Trusts

"Love believes all things." This verse does not mean that we should naively believe everything that anyone tells us. Perhaps we have heard a false rumor or a lie. Or maybe false doctrine is being taught. We need to learn to be discerning. "Dear friends, do not believe every spirit, but test the spirits to see whether they are from God, because many false prophets have gone out into the world" (1 John 4:1).

Believing all things means we believe that our fellow Christians have the ability to choose to do what is right. Love looks for the best, not the worst, in others, believing there is hope for us all. Other people may not do right every time (do we?), but we trust that they have the ability to improve. Love believes that when any of us sins, we can repent and return to God. After all, God is still working on all of us. We want others to believe in us, so we should believe in them and encourage them. As we encourage others, God uses us to change lives. We all need someone who believes in us, who is in our corner to help us when we need it, to pray for us, to lead us closer to God, to stick with us no matter how bad we are.

If we do not believe in God, then we have no basis for belief in others. Love believes in God and in his promises to us. Without his grace, none of us could hope for the forgiveness he offers us. We need forgiveness for ourselves as much as we need to forgive others. If we do not believe that sinners can improve, then we will not forgive them. And if we do not forgive, then we will not be forgiven (Matt. 6:14–15). If we do not have a good relationship with God, we will not have a good relationship with others (1 John 4:20–21).

Love Always Hopes

When love trusts that Christians have the ability to choose to do right, then love *hopes* that they will choose the right. And after they have chosen rightly, love trusts and hopes that they will indeed continue in the right.

Biblical hope is more than merely a wish. When we say, "I hope I get a letter tomorrow," we know we may or we may not get the wished-for letter. But biblical hope is a firm conviction that we have adequate reason for confidence in what we hope for, even though we have not yet experienced the conclusion. For instance, we have hope that the sun will rise tomorrow. We have not yet seen that particular sunrise, but we have experienced enough sunrises that we have confidence it will happen again tomorrow.

Hebrews 11:1 relates faith and hope: "Now faith is being sure of what we hope for and certain of what we do not see." There is no uncertainty in either faith or hope. The rest of Hebrews 11 illustrates in the lives of Old Testament characters how they lived faithfully in hope as they followed God's will, even though they did not live to see the final fulfillment of God's promises. They were confident of the outcome.

We, too, can be sure that God will keep his promises to us, and that should make us want to keep our promises to fellow Christians. We have confidence that anyone who is following Jesus has the ability to obey his will in their lives. Of course, all of us will fall short of perfection, but love wants us to turn back to God and be forgiven of our sins. God has given us many assurances that we can hope for salvation if we obey him.

The focus of hope in 1 Corinthians 13 is on what people can become, and relationships are sustained by a love that never lets others down—because "Love never fails" (1 Cor. 13:8).

Love Always Perseveres

Some translations say, "Love bears all things." Others say, "Love endures all things." There is a distinction between the meanings of "bears all things" and "endures all things" even though they are closely related.

> "Endures" seems to imply a period of time more than "bears" does. "Bears all things" does indicate a loving attitude must be exhibited as long as a problem exists. But "endures" implies a long-time perseverance and patience. Some suggest that "bears" describes the initial attitude toward another person, while "endures" describes the continuation of that attitude. "Bears" is like starting the car and leaving the driveway, while "endures" is like driving all the way to the destination.[9]

God's love is everlasting, and ours should be also. He loves us no matter how many times we sin and ask for his forgiveness. God sets no limit on forgiveness. Therefore, we cannot set limits on how long we will keep on enduring a fellow Christian's problems. We will love that person enough to give our help no matter how many times he or she stumbles.

Challenge Yourself

To see what a challenge it is to live a life of love as described in 1 Corinthians 13, put your own name in the place of the word "love." "*Nancy* is patient. *Nancy* is kind," etc. As we put ourselves beside the ideal that God has put before us in his Word, we see how far we fall behind. But we can be thankful that he has given us the goal toward which we can work.

We know that God is on our side, that he rejoices with us when we do right and weeps over us when we sin. It is his love and mercy that support us in our daily lives as we try to live for him. It is for the love of the Lord, both his love for us and our love for him, that we can endure the hardships of this life and look forward to the glories of the future world in heaven with God. "Be faithful, even to the point of death, and I will give you the crown of life" (Rev. 2:10b).

Love Never Ends

I am reminded of the song "Tie a Yellow Ribbon 'Round the Old Oak Tree," about a young man who had done wrong and spent time in jail. He had been released and was on his way to the town in which his family lived. He did not know how they would receive him. He was afraid that he had behaved so badly that they would not want him to come home again. So he had written them that he would be on the bus that day. If it was all right for him to come home, they could tie a yellow ribbon on the oak tree at the edge of the town. If he saw the yellow ribbon, he would get off the bus and come home. But if there was no yellow ribbon on the tree, then he would stay on the bus and they would never be bothered by him again. As the bus neared the bend in the road just before the tree, the young man was very nervous. Would there be a ribbon on the tree or not? Would he ever see his family again? He was worried. However as the tree came into view, everyone on the bus saw that huge yellow ribbons were tied on every branch of the tree, and they all cheered! The tree was completely covered with bright yellow ribbons! His family loved him enough to give him a second chance. Their love for him never ended.[10]

The story in this song reminds me of the love that God has for us. It never ends. He always gives us a second chance (or third, or fourth, or 490th!—see Matt. 18:22 KJV) to repent and get it right. What a wonderful blessing that is to us! We can cheer along with those on the bus when we see someone who has repented, has been forgiven, and is receiving another chance. It is an even greater blessing when we are the forgiven ones.

We could study love without ever coming to the end of it, because love never ends. We could practice love all our lives and we would never get it entirely right, but we should keep on trying. Love never ends because God is love and God is eternal—therefore love is also eternal.

Faith and hope will end, but love never will. Faith and hope will be unnecessary when our faith becomes sight and our hope is realized. Thus Paul says that love is the greatest of these three (v. 13). Love will triumph over everything and will last for eternity. Heaven is what it is by the presence of God. Therefore heaven will be filled with love and there will be no selfishness and no envy, no boasting, no arrogance, no rudeness, no anger, no keeping records of wrong, no delight in evil. Our finite minds cannot fathom the extent of that love. It is greater than anything we can imagine. However, as we try to live for the love of the Lord, we will grow in our ability to understand. And someday, we will know fully the love that God has for us. In our lives on this earth, we do not know fully what this kind of love really is, but we can say with Paul, "Now I know in part; then I shall know fully, even as I am fully known" (1 Cor. 13:12b).

Because God, our father, loves us, he wants us to get along with each other. He wants peace among his children. He is the God of peace, and through Jesus, he will supply us with everything we need to be pleasing to him. My prayer for you is the same as that of the writer of Hebrews:

> May the God of peace, who through the blood of the eternal covenant brought back from the dead our Lord Jesus, that great Shepherd of the sheep, equip you with everything good for doing his will, and may he work in us what is pleasing to him, through Jesus Christ, to whom be glory for ever and ever. Amen." (13:20–21)

---FOR FURTHER THOUGHT---

1. Which of the characteristics of love in 1 Corinthians 13 means the most to you?

2. Why is that characteristic of love so important to you?

3. Which characteristics of love do you need to work on the most in your life?

4. What will you do to improve those aspects of love in your life?

5. How can you train your children (or grandchildren, or others) to know this kind of love and how to make it a part of their lives?

Chapter Eleven

LOVE SERVES

"Serve one another in love."
—Galatians 5:13

When you ask children what they want to be when they grow up, rarely will you hear one of them say, "I want to be a *servant*!" They do not aspire to being servants, probably because society in general looks upon a servant as an inferior person. This way of thinking has rubbed off onto the children, and they have concluded that being a servant is not a good goal for their lives.

However, is that the way the Lord thinks? Not at all. Jesus told his disciples that he came not to be served, but to serve (Matt. 20:25–28). We might say that he is the master servant. Jesus, their master, certainly was not inferior to his disciples, yet he willingly and lovingly became their servant. He told them to follow his example in serving others. Likewise, we today should also follow his example.

The New Testament makes obvious that *agape* love should be an essential part of our lives ("Do everything in love" [1 Cor. 16:14]) and that such love includes service ("Serve one another in love" [Gal. 5:13c]). The New Testament also gives us examples of many men and women who served the Lord and their fellow Christians with love. In most cases, we are not told exactly what these people did. We often wish that we knew more about them and their activities. However, God has told us what we need to know, including some of the things we can do to serve others.

Jesus Set an Example of Service

As the apostles were arguing with each other about which one of them was the greatest, Jesus told them that the greatest is the one who serves.

> Jesus said to them, "The kings of the Gentiles lord it over them; and those who exercise authority over them call themselves Benefactors. But you are not to be like that. Instead, the greatest among you should be like the youngest and the one who rules like the one who serves. For who is greater, the one who is at the table or the one who serves? Is it not the one who is at the table? But I am among you as one who serves. (Luke 22:25-27)

Jesus set an example for us of service to others. If we want to be like him, we will gladly humble ourselves and serve our fellow Christians in whatever way we can, without insisting on the "better" jobs. When Jesus washed the feet of his disciples (John 13:4-5), he was doing the job of the lowliest slave in a household, thus showing us that nothing should be too menial for us to do. If it needs to be done, do it humbly and lovingly.

A number of years ago, my family attended a congregation in Athens, Greece, composed mainly of military personnel. One Sunday, as a major was leaving the assembly of the church, he noticed that a sergeant's car had a flat tire. Without hesitation, the major changed the tire on the sergeant's car. In the military, that is not the way things usually work. But the major was a willing servant who was showing his love both for the sergeant and for the Lord.

Both Men and Women Serve

As Christians we are "created for good deeds" or "good works" (Eph. 2:8-10). This "we" includes both men and women. Unfortunately, some women today feel left out when they see some things that men are doing to serve the Lord. They think that they should be allowed to do anything and everything that the men do. And they argue with the Lord about his commands. Do they think the Lord did not mean what he said?

Serving with love applies to both men and women, but because women sometimes feel inferior or secondary in the church, the focus of this chapter will be on women and their service to the Lord.

Although there are some restrictions that God himself has placed on women,[1] there are many things that women can do. The restrictions that God commanded mainly concern women in the assembly of his church (1 Cor. 14:33–37). Actually, there is so much for women to do in service to the Lord besides preaching and praying in the assembly that there is no way anyone can do everything in one lifetime.

Let me emphasize that the restriction on women's speech in the assembly of the church has nothing whatsoever to do with women being in submission to men and their decisions (as many people think), but it has everything to do with women being in submission to God. The silence of women in the assembly of the church is not the result of a decision made by men, but it is a direct command of God (1 Cor. 14:37). And it is a command that must be taken very seriously.

Women in the New Testament

Many of the things that women do are the same that all Christians do: both men and women assemble together, worship together, live worthy lives, and do good deeds for others. However, there are some passages in Scripture addressed specifically to women (including 1 Tim. 2:9–15 and Titus 2:3–5). And I am convinced that there are some things that women can do better than men. Sometimes a woman's touch is needed. Throughout the centuries, the church of our Lord has profited from the actions of devoted female members.

The New Testament tells us of a number of women who worked hard for the Lord. We will mention only a few of them. Perhaps that will show us some things that women can do to follow God's will and live for the love of the Lord.

- Mary's faith and her submissive attitude should be an inspiration to all of us. Would that we could all "find favor with the Lord" as she did (Luke 1:27, 30, 38).
- Anna was devoted in worshiping God night and day, in the temple with prayer and fasting (Luke 2:36–37).
- When Peter's mother-in-law was healed, she got up and served her guests (Matt. 8:14–15).
- The woman who had been bleeding for twelve years had faith in Jesus's power and she acted on that faith (Matt. 9:20–22; Mark 5:25; Luke 8:43).
- The Canaanite woman had such great faith that she was persistent, and so Jesus granted her request (Matt. 15:21–28; Mark 7:24–30).
- Mary gave excellent advice for all of us when she told the stewards at Cana, "Do whatever Jesus tells you" (John 2:5).
- The mother of James and John was bold enough to go to Jesus with her special request (as misguided as it was—Matt. 20:20–22).
- The Samaritan woman was busy doing what we all should be doing—telling friends and neighbors about the Lord. She was evangelizing (John 4:28–30, 39).
- The poor widow gave so generously that Jesus commended her (Mark 12:42–44; Luke 21:1–4).
- Several women traveled with Jesus and his disciples to care for their needs by supporting them out of their own means (Matt. 27:55–56; Luke 8:1–3).
- Then there were Mary and Martha, busy serving and learning (Luke 10:38–42). At the death of their brother, they showed their faith in Jesus, as Martha confessed, "I believe that you are the Christ, the Son of God, who was to come into the world" (John 11:27).
- Women were the first to go to the tomb early on Sunday morning to care for his body (Matt. 28:1; Mark 16:1; Luke 24:1–11; John 20:1–18).

- Dorcas "was always doing good and helping the poor" (Acts 9:36–43).
- Mary, John Mark's mother, opened her home as a place where the Christians could meet to pray (Acts 12:12–17).
- Timothy's mother and his grandmother taught him Scripture from a very early age (Acts 16:1; 2 Tim. 1:5; 3:15).
- Lydia heard the gospel and immediately obeyed it. Then she showed her hospitality to Paul and his company and also allowed the church to meet in her home (Acts 16:13–15, 40).
- Priscilla worked beside her husband in their business, while opening their home to Paul. She also worked with Aquila in teaching Apollos "the way of God more adequately" (Acts 18:2–3, 24–26).
- In Romans 16, Paul greets several women by name, saying that they worked hard in the Lord. I especially like what he said about Rufus's mother, "Who has been a mother to me, too" (v. 13). I really would like to know just what she did for Paul that made him feel so close to her. I am sure that many who are reading this have done similar things to encourage and strengthen the faith of many.

And I could go on, as there are many other women mentioned in the New Testament.

Women in Church History

The activities and influence of women in the church did not end with the first century. Throughout the ages, women have been important in the furtherance of the gospel—not by preaching from the pulpit, but in many other ways:

> The lives of women may not be covered extensively in the surviving literature of the early church, but women certainly were prominent in its story. The names of only a few are known, but the *numbers* of women believers were greater than those of male believers....

> Some of the most heroic martyrs of the early church were women.... Women were also involved in the missionary outreach of the gospel, accompanying apostles and evangelists on their travels and working in the women's quarters of households to which men did not have access.... Despite the feeling of some that women were untrustworthy teachers, they were often engaged in private teaching.... New Testament strictures against women doing public teaching in church, and against women filling the position of elders, seem to have been uniformly observed in the mainstream of the church.[2]

To learn more about the other ways in which women have served, we will consider a few of the women from early church history and what they did.

Not very many women are named until about the fourth century, except for some martyrs. There are very moving accounts of some of these women who died because of their love for the Lord. One of those women was Blandina, who was martyred at Lyon, France, in 177. A fairly large number of Christians was martyred at about the same time. Eusebius, an early church historian, is the source of the text that described what happened:

> All of us were in terror; and Blandina's earthly mistress, who was herself among the martyrs in the conflict, was in agony lest because of her bodily weakness she would not be able to make a bold confession of her faith. Yet Blandina was filled with such power that even those who were taking turns to torture her in every way from dawn to dusk were weary and exhausted. They themselves admitted that they were beaten, that there was nothing further they could do to her, and they were surprised that she was still breathing, for her entire body was broken and torn. They testified that even one kind of torture was enough to release her soul, let alone the many they applied with such intensity. Instead, this blessed woman like a noble athlete got renewed strength with her confession of faith: her admission, "I am a Christian; we do nothing to be ashamed of," brought her refreshment, rest, and insensibility to her present pain....
>
> [T]iny, weak, and insignificant as she was she would give inspiration to her brothers, for she had put on Christ, that mighty and invincible athlete, and had overcome the Adversary

in many contests, and through her conflict had won the crown of immortality.³

We can learn much from the martyrs about faith and faithfulness until death, though we hope we do not need to face that kind of persecution in our lives. However, in various parts of the world, people are being killed for their faith even today.

We can also learn from women who were not martyred, but served the Lord in various ways. As we look at four of the named women from the fourth century, I hope you can see some things that these women did that we, too, can do today as we serve one another with love.

- **Nonna** was the Mother of Gregory of Nazianzus and lived from 300 to 374. She "was the wife, mother, and grandmother of bishops.... Her husband's conversion was her doing. Gregory attributes this to her prayers, her pleadings, and above all the influence of her character." Her husband later became bishop of Nazianzus. "Her significant contribution of piety and business skill was surpassed only by the influence for good she had on her family and through them on others."⁴

- **Anthusa** was the mother of John Chrysostom and lived in the late fourth century. Widowed at the age of twenty with an infant to raise, "she refused all offers of marriage and dedicated herself to the rearing of her son." She taught him "to know and to love the Scriptures." And so John became "one of the greatest expository preachers of all time," so great that he received the nickname "Chrysostom," which means "Golden Mouth." When John's teacher, a non-Christian, learned about Anthusa, her activities, her piety, and her character, he commented, "'What women these Christians have!' Here was pagan testimony to a significant channel of the power of Christianity. Through its women who had given themselves selflessly to their responsibilities, the church had attained its position in the world."⁵

- **Macrina** was the sister of two of the most influential men of the fourth-century church—Gregory of Nyssa and Basil the Great. She lived from 327 to 380, and she "was largely responsible for what [Gregory and Basil] became." After her father's death, she decided never to marry but to devote herself to helping her mother raise her nine younger siblings. "She became the leading spiritual influence in a family that was to take a prominent place in church affairs in the late fourth century.... Her practical piety, intelligence, and strength of personality had made her the dominant spirit in an influential family."[6]

- **Marcella** was a Roman noblewoman drawn to Christianity by the fourth-century biblical scholar Jerome, and she was "especially notable as a student and teacher." She held Bible studies in her home and converted others. "Among her benefactions was the support of the studies and writing done by Jerome, who was one of many dependent on the favor of wealthy women for their scholarly endeavors."[7]

"Devotion to family, faithfulness to the church, study of Scripture, charitable use of possessions: these are some of the outstanding qualities that seem to be shared by the great women of the ancient church."[8]

There are many things that women can do in service to the Lord. The writer of Hebrews mentions some things that Christians, both men and women (the word "brothers" in this passage includes women), can and should be doing: "Keep on loving each other as brothers. Do not forget to entertain strangers, for by so doing some people have entertained angels without knowing it. Remember those in prison as if you were their fellow prisoners, and those who are mistreated as if you yourselves were suffering" (Heb. 13:1–3). My prayer is that you will find many ways of serving the Lord with love and according to his will.

---FOR FURTHER THOUGHT---

1. What are some things that women did in New Testament times to show their love for the Lord?

2. What are some things that women in church history did in service to the church and to the Lord?

3. What are some things that women can do today to show their love for the Lord?

4. When and how should women follow God's command in 1 Corinthians 14:33–38?

CHAPTER TWELVE

A LOVING SERVANT

"I commend to you our sister Phoebe."
—ROMANS 16:1

In the previous chapter, we looked at what some women did for the love of the Lord in the early centuries of the church. Now, as we turn back to the New Testament, we take Phoebe as an example of a woman who did many good works because of her faith and love.

At the end of his letter to the church at Rome, Paul sends personal greetings to several individual Christians. He also introduces and recommends to them Phoebe, whose name is the first to be mentioned in Romans 16. All we know about this woman is what Paul told the Romans, yet we can learn some important things from these few lines: "I commend to you our sister Phoebe, a servant of the church in Cenchreae. I ask you to receive her in the Lord in a way worthy of the saints and to give her any help she may need from you, for she has been a great help to many people, including me" (Rom. 16:1–2).

INTRODUCING PHOEBE

The first thing we learn is this woman's name. Not every woman, nor even every man, mentioned in the Bible was named. For some reason, Phoebe was important enough to be singled out. Paul mentioned a number of persons by name in this chapter, several of whom were women, but Phoebe was different from the others. Paul was not greeting her; rather, he was introducing her to the Christians in Rome. Later, we shall see why it was important for her to have this introduction.

The Family of God

We also learn that Phoebe was a Christian. The literal translation is "our sister." Her love for God caused Phoebe to dedicate her life to Christ and to doing God's will. Not only was she Paul's sister, and the Roman Christians' sister, but she was our sister as well. As Christians, we have a special kinship with her through Christ. We have the same kinship with her across the centuries that we have across the miles with our fellow Christians in Africa, Asia, Europe, and other places around the world. We need to remember all our brothers and sisters in Christ, wherever they are, because they are our spiritual family.

The Christian family is very important, especially when one is away from home and familiar faces. Anyone who has spent time on a foreign mission field can attest to the importance of being with fellow Christians any time the opportunity arises.

Ancient Hospitality

Phoebe was in need of Christian hospitality. Why? Because she was traveling, and modern accommodations for travelers were not available. Why was she traveling? Although we do not know for sure, perhaps it was because of private business, or perhaps it was on behalf of the church of which she was a servant. Perhaps it was even for the purpose of delivering Paul's letter to the Romans; but if so, there probably would have been some additional reason for her traveling to Rome.

Ancient Mail Service

Most likely, Phoebe was going to Rome for reasons of her own, and since she was going, Paul sent the letter with her. We may complain about the U.S. Postal Service, but at least we have easy access to it. However, in imperial Rome, the mails were reserved for official business (administrative, military, and diplomatic communications). Private citizens had to depend on slaves, employees, or friends to take their letters to the proper destination.[1]

Whatever her reasons, Phoebe was traveling to Rome, and Paul wanted the Christians there to know that she, too, was a Christian and deserved the warm reception one experiences within a loving family. Thus Paul gave a glowing introduction of her to the church in Rome and asked them to help her in any way they could, especially in ways that she had probably often helped others. There are many examples in ancient literature of such letters of introduction. In his commentary on Romans, C. H. Dodd mentions letters of this type:

> The terms in which Paul writes are familiar from examples of letters of introduction among papyri of the period. Such letters of introduction were evidently widely used among the early Christian communities.... The necessity of a proper introduction for persons less well known ... is obvious. A church must know that a stranger arriving and seeking hospitality as a fellow-Christian is a genuine member of the Christian society, and not a parasite or a spy. In a satirical work of the second century [*De Morte Peregrini*, attributed to Lucian of Samosata] there is an amusing account of how an impostor made a very good thing out of the generosity of simple and credulous Christian communities.[2]

So we see the necessity of Paul's introduction of Phoebe to the Romans. Even today, it is sometimes important for churches to receive such letters.

Travel in Phoebe's Time

We have often heard about the fine roads built by the Romans, but what about accommodations for those traveling? In *Backgrounds of Early Christianity*, Everett Ferguson discussed travel in Phoebe's time:

> The traveler was not so fortunate in the accommodations for the night as he was in the quality of the roads on which he traveled by day. Not that inns were lacking, but their reputation (in quality and morals) was notorious.... The upper classes avoided the

public accommodations and stayed with friends when they traveled. The moral dangers at the inns made hospitality an important virtue in early Christianity. Hospitality occupies a prominent place in Christian literature ... because of the needs of missionaries and messengers of the churches and other Christians who happened to be traveling. The churches provided an extended family, giving lodging and assistance for the journey. Christians here followed and expanded a Jewish practice of caring for their own away from home.... Many synagogues had guest rooms attached for the use of Jews on a journey.[3]

Paul may have been asking the Romans to do for Phoebe what she had done for many others. Cenchreae, her home, was a port city near Corinth, and Phoebe may have extended hospitality many times to fellow Christians who were traveling.

Welcome

Phoebe was worthy of the best reception they could give her. Paul wanted a good reception for Phoebe's sake, but he knew that it would also be a benefit to the church in Rome. Different translations give slightly different wordings of verse 2: "Welcome her in the Lord as is fitting for the saints" (NRSV); "receive her in the Lord in a way worthy of the saints" (NIV); and "I ask you to accept her in the Lord. Accept her the way God's people should" (ERV). In other words, "Receive her in a way that shows you are God's people, because she, too, is a sister in Christ."

Suppose the leaders in the congregation you attend received a letter introducing someone with credentials similar to Phoebe's. Wouldn't it show a lack of spiritual discernment if the church ignored that person? We can show our love to God by helping a fellow Christian. Jesus himself said, "I tell you the truth, whatever you did for one of the least of these brothers of mine, you did for me" (Matt. 25:40).

The Romans needed to give Phoebe a good reception as surely as she needed to receive it. The kind of reception Paul wanted was as valuable for them as it was for her. And we need to remember that as we help others.

Patrons

Phoebe was a *prostatis*, a "benefactor" or "patroness" of many. This means she was probably fairly wealthy. We do not know if she was a business woman, like Lydia, or if her husband (who is not mentioned) provided the standard of living that enabled her to help others. But we do know a little about patrons in the ancient society:

> A regular code of etiquette governed the duty ... of a client to the patron.... The client was responsible for assisting the patron in political and private life and for showing respect by walking in the funeral procession.... The patron's role was to give a small dole of gifts or money. The patron rendered assistance in need, welcomed the client from time to time to his house and table, and offered legal protection as needed. The relationship operated on all levels and in various groupings: between former masters and freedmen, rich and poor, generals and conquered peoples, aristocrats and *collegia* or clubs....
>
> Phoebe, the servant of the church at Cenchreae, is described as a patroness (Rom. 16:2), one who gives aid and who had the resources to do so.[4]

"Women in the early Roman empire in practice were more prominent than some ancient texts would indicate. Wealth and social position made some women patrons and gave them considerable power and influence apart from the social theory of the time."[5]

Phoebe may or may not have been a "patron" in the technical sense of the word, but Paul does say that she helped "many, including myself," so she must have served others by doing many good things for many different people.

House Churches

One way that Phoebe may have served the church as a patron was to allow the church to meet in her home. The early church did not have church buildings as we know them today. They usually met in small groups in homes. We see this in those passages in which Paul mentions "the church that meets at their house": Romans 16:5, 1 Corinthians 16:19, Colossians

4:15, and Philemon 2. These groups are today generally called "house churches."

It was not until about the end of the third century or the beginning of the fourth that Christians began erecting special buildings in which to meet, even though there is evidence that earlier there were some houses converted into meeting places:

> The earliest evidence of a house converted architecturally into a place of Christian worship is from Dura-Europos, dated ca. 241–256. It is a typical house with rooms grouped around a central court. It is significant, however, that at this conversion all domestic functions ceased, and the building was given over completely to religious use, it was a "church building."[6]

Servant? Deacon? Minister?

Before we go to the next description of Phoebe, let me ask you to put on your "thinking cap." Perhaps the following will help your understanding of what we will discuss next.

Think of a man in your home congregation who is often busy volunteering to do things for the church that need to be done. Any time he sees something that needs to be done, he quietly gets busy and does it. Can we call him a "servant" of the church?

Now think of a woman who, in the same way, is often busy doing whatever needs to be done for the church. Can she also be called a "servant" of the church?

When we call someone a servant of the church, we are not just saying this person has done certain specific things. Rather, we mean that this person has a servant attitude—that he or she is willing to do whatever needs to be done.

Now, think of a man who is a "deacon" in your home congregation. What does that mean? A deacon is someone who has been called out by the church and appointed by the elders to do certain jobs. Perhaps the elders have appointed a woman to a certain job, such as supervising children's classes. This woman could also be called a "deacon" in connection with this work. This is a job she has been given to do for the church, whether she has the designation "deaconess" or not. We will discuss this more later.

Next, think of the man who usually delivers the sermon. Probably he is referred to as the "minister" of the church, meaning that he is the preacher. However, there are ways of ministering other than being in the pulpit on Sunday morning.

What would you think if I said, "*You* are a minister of the church"?

Several years ago, our congregation had a display board with individual pictures of all the members. The caption over the pictures said, "The ministers of the Hillcrest church." That was meant to indicate that all members should be ministering in some way to others. "Minister" is not necessarily a technical, specialized term. It is not limited in meaning to "one who preaches." It should apply to all of us as we serve and help others.

As you read Romans 16:1–2 from the following translations, notice the different ways of translating two of the words that describe Phoebe:

> I commend to you our sister Phoebe, a <u>servant</u> of the church in Cenchreae. I ask you to receive her in the Lord in a way worthy of the saints and to give her any help she may need from you, for she has been a great help to many people, including me. (NIV).

> I commend to you our sister Phoebe, a <u>deacon</u> of the church at Cenchreae, so that you may welcome her in the Lord as is fitting for the saints, and help her in whatever she may require from you, for she has been a <u>benefactor</u> of many and of myself as well. (NRSV)

The Revised English Bible renders these two words as <u>minister</u> and <u>good friend</u>. But perhaps the translation by Conybeare and Howson best conveys the meaning when it says, "who is a <u>ministering servant</u> of the Church … she <u>has</u> herself <u>aided</u> many."[7]

Now you see some of the problems involved in translating ancient languages into modern speech. How do you translate what Paul was saying in the first century into what we are hearing in the twenty-first century? "Minister" gives a wrong impression to us today, even though it is a correct translation. We think of a "preacher" or "hired professional." A nurse's ministering to her patients carries a more accurate meaning. "Deacon" also gives the impression of an official office. We will consider this further as we continue. "Servant" is probably not as strong a word for us as Paul intended based on the rest of his description of Phoebe, especially "patron." But what was Phoebe? Servant? Deacon? Minister? With proper understanding, she was all three.

Diakonos

We need to look further at the meaning of *diakonos*. Just what did that word mean when Paul wrote it? According to one lexicon, *diakonos* refers to "1. one who serves as an intermediary in a transaction, *agent, intermediary, courier*" and "2. one who gets something done, at the behest of a superior, *assistant* to someone."[8] Another lexicon defines this word as "servant" or "messenger."[9] Thus we see that *diakonos* meant one who ministers, attends, serves, helps, delivers a message for. It referred to a servant, minister, attendant, or helper. It involved active service. It did not refer to a servant who was a slave in relation to a person (there was another word for that relationship—*doulos*), but to a person who was a servant in relation to a work or specific job. It meant one who renders service, who performs an assigned task.

The New Testament uses *diakonos* in several different situations, referring to various persons. Perhaps looking at some who are described by this word will help us better to understand the meaning of it. Here are some in the New Testament described by the word *diakonos*:

1. Christ in Romans 15:8: "For I tell you that Christ has become a servant [*diakonos*] of the Jews on behalf of God's truth, to confirm the promises made to the patriarchs."

2. Apostles in Matthew 20:26: "Not so with you. Instead, whoever wants to become great among you must be your servant [*diakonos*]."
3. Evangelists in 1 Timothy 4:6: "If you point these things out to the brothers, you will be a good minister [*diakonos*] of Christ Jesus, brought up in the truths of the faith and of the good teaching that you have followed."
4. Christians in John 12:26: "Whoever serves [*diakoneo*—verb form] me must follow me; and where I am, my servant [*diakonos*] also will be. My Father will honor the one who serves [*diakoneo*] me."
5. Civil Magistrate in Romans 13:4: "For he is God's servant [*diakonos*] to do you good. But if you do wrong, be afraid, for he does not bear the sword for nothing. He is God's servant [*diakonos*], an agent of wrath to bring punishment on the wrongdoer."
6. Emissaries of Satan in 2 Corinthians 11:15: "It is not surprising, then, if his servants [*diakonos*] masquerade as servants [*diakonos*] of righteousness. Their end will be what their actions deserve."
7. Waiters at festivals in John 2:5: "His mother said to the servants [*diakonos*], 'Do whatever he tells you.'"
8. Church leaders in Philippians 1:1: "Paul and Timothy, servants [*doulos*] of Christ Jesus, To all the saints in Christ Jesus at Philippi, together with the overseers and deacons [*diakonos*]"; and 1 Timothy 3:8: "Deacons [*diakonos*], likewise, are to be men worthy of respect, sincere, not indulging in much wine, and not pursuing dishonest gain."

Thus we see that this word *diakonos* has many uses besides its reference to the office of deacon as described in 1 Timothy 3:8. For example, the word "deacon" is used to describe the Civil Magistrate in Romans 13:4, but it does not mean that he was a deacon in the church. One cannot claim that every time that word is used, it must refer to the office of deacon in the church.

Because the one Greek word *(diakonos)* can be translated by three English words (minister, servant, and deacon), we might say that Phoebe was a ministering servant who had been given a task (or tasks) to do for the church.

Women as Deacons

Much discussion occurs concerning whether or not women can be deacons in an official sense. First Timothy 3:11 is at the heart of that discussion: "Women [or wives] likewise must be serious, not slanderers, but temperate, faithful in all things" (RSV). This is a passage in which the Greek is ambiguous and therefore the English should also be ambiguous. The Greek word for "women" is the same as the word for "wives." Such translations as "Their wives" (NIV) or "The deaconesses"[10] are misleading. These are commentaries, not accurate translations. The translators have tried to clarify the verse, but in doing so, they have chosen wording that reflects their own opinions. Again, if the Greek is ambiguous, the English translation should be also.

As Dodd said, "It would be interesting to know more of Phoebe and of her place and functions in the church of Cenchreae, but we are ill informed about the ministry of women in the early Church. The term by which she is described ... is a very general term."[11]

The discussion of Phoebe as a deacon in the same sense as the men in 1 Timothy has generally neglected a verse that must be included: "A deacon must be the husband of but one wife" (1 Tim. 3:12). A literal translation in both verse 12 and verse 2 is "a one-woman man." Phoebe, therefore, was probably not a deacon in an official sense. However, if she was, we should remember that the office of deacon is not a position of authority but of service. The deacons serve the church under the supervision of its overseers, the elders.

Because the overwhelming majority of uses of *diakonos* is in a non-technical, general descriptive sense, Phoebe was probably a ministering servant of the church without a title. The text does not give us the content of her service, but it may have included some of the activities mentioned above. As a patroness, benefactor, and helper, she used her resources and influence on behalf of the church and in assistance to others.

Conclusion

We all, both men and women, need to be doing as much as we can to further the work of the church. We should not care if we have the title or not; we just want to work for the Lord! We should be ministers, servants, and deacons. I am not saying that we need to have women "ministers" in the sense of a preacher, or that we need to have women "deacons" in an official capacity. Many women have been leaders in the Lord's church and yet have stayed within the bounds of God's word. Women can and should do much in loving service to our Lord and Master. Unfortunately, they have sometimes been held back by a false sense of not being permitted to do anything. Yes, there are some restrictions on women, but not as many as has been thought. Women can do much good as ministering servants.

Let me encourage you to read and study the Bible and then to go out and do all the good works you can for the love of the Lord. Serve him and the people around you wholeheartedly and to the best of your God-given abilities.

Phoebe must have had great love for her Lord as well as for the members of his church to spend her life as a servant, a minister, and a deacon. She set a good example for all of us.

My prayer is that all of us, with great joy, will glorify God, praising him and recognize his authority in everything, as we obey and serve him in love. Then we can say with Jude, "To him who is able to keep you from falling and to present you before his glorious presence without fault and with great joy—to the only God our Savior be glory, majesty, power and authority, through Jesus Christ our Lord, before all ages, now and forevermore! Amen" (v. 24–25).

---FOR FURTHER THOUGHT---

1. Why did Phoebe need the introduction that Paul gave her to the Roman Christians?

2. Why was hospitality important in New Testament times?

3. Is hospitality still important today? Why?

4. What is the difference in meaning between "servant," "minister," and "deacon" in New Testament times and today?

5. What attitude should women have toward serving in the church?

Chapter Thirteen

Love Is the Answer

"Love comes from God."
—1 John 4:7

We have defined love, discussed how God shows his love to us, and considered how we show our love to him. We have seen how love applies to husbands and wives, parents and children, and among all Christians. We have noted how God treats us as his children, lavishing love on us and protecting us from evil. And we have looked at someone who served her fellow Christians and her Lord with love.

All this is for the love of the Lord—both his love for us and our love for him.

Now, what does this mean to the way we live day-by-day?

Love Transforms

Can love transform us? What do we become when that love transforms us? Years ago, I knew a man who was a typical confirmed bachelor. He had no plans ever to get married. However, he met a lady who quickly unconfirmed him! They fell in love, and he no longer wanted to be a bachelor. She did not force him to change; it was his love for her and her love for him that transformed him from a bachelor into a loving husband. Love made him want to spend the rest of his life with her.

Perhaps you know a couple that has been married for fifty or sixty years and both are still in love with each other. They have probably become more alike as the years have passed. They did not force change on each other, but love transformed them into better spouses as they learned to live a life of love. And it all started with loving actions.

In the same way, as we spend time falling in love with the Lord, we will become more like him. God will not force us to change, but the love of the Lord will transform us into being better servants for him. As we learn more of his love for us, we will love him more, also.

Love Saves

God has acted in many loving ways toward us. Some of these we should immediately recognize as coming from God. For example, he created the beautiful night sky that declares his glory (Ps. 19:1–4). We should recognize the eternal power and divine nature of God from what he has made (Rom. 1:19-20).

However, other loving acts may not be recognized by us as coming from God until he reveals himself. An example of this is found in John 3:16: "For God so loved the world that he gave his one and only Son, that whoever believes in him shall not perish but have eternal life." Jesus is a blessing that we would not recognize as coming from God without the revelations found in God's word, the Bible.

The Bible is where we are told about the wonderful love God has for us. If God had not loved us so much, we would not know the saving love that he bestows on us daily. We would not know his grace, which gives us the opportunity of eternal life with God in heaven. According to John 3:16, only those who believe in the Lord will receive eternal life. However, this belief is more than merely saying, "Oh, yes, I believe there is a God somewhere."

Saving belief includes trust and obedience. That is, if we believe that Jesus is truly the Son of the living God, we will trust him completely. If we trust him, we will obey God's commands to the best of our abilities.

As we learn to trust him more and to obey him better, we realize that he always keeps his promises. When we believe, when we are convinced that he will keep his promises (Rom. 4:20–21), then we can have confidence in our salvation. First John tells us, "I write these things to you who believe in the name of the Son of God so that you may know that you have eternal life" (5:13).

We need to know the truths about God and Jesus revealed to us in the Bible. We also need to love God's truth to the extent that we live by it. We cannot do anything to earn or deserve our salvation, but we can act in such a way that we will lose that salvation: "They perish because they refused to love the truth and so be saved" (2 Thess. 2:10b). We should recognize the importance not only of knowing the facts about God, but also of knowing the Lord himself and believing on the Lord Jesus Christ. If we have faith and confidence in the Lord, then we will show that faith by our actions (James 2:18–19). We cannot separate faith from obedience. Living our faith will determine how we act day by day:

> We know that we have come to know him if we obey his commands. The man who says, "I know him," but does not do what he commands is a liar, and the truth is not in him. But if anyone obeys his word, God's love is truly made complete in him. This is how we know we are in him: Whoever claims to live in him must walk as Jesus did. (1 John 2:3–6)

Love Leads the Way

Jesus showed his great love for us by coming to earth and willingly dying for us, to purify us from our sins: "It was just before the Passover Feast. Jesus knew that the time had come for him to leave this world and go to the Father. Having loved his own who were in the world, he now showed them the full extent of his love" (John 13:1). Jesus then washed his disciple's feet as an act of humble service, to set an example for their service. However, the full extent of his love for us is shown in his willing death.

Yet dying for us was not enough. It was also necessary for him to be raised from the dead. Without his resurrection, we would have no hope of heaven. Paul assures us that the resurrection of Jesus leads the way for our future resurrection.

> I want to remind you of the gospel I preached to you, which you received.... By this gospel you are saved, if you hold firmly to the word I preached to you. Otherwise, you have believed in vain.
>
> For what I received I passed on to you as of first importance: that Christ died for our sins according to the Scriptures, that he was buried, that he was raised on the third day according to the Scriptures, and that he appeared to Peter, and then to the Twelve.... (1 Cor. 15:1–5)

and

> He was delivered over to death for our sins and was raised to life for our justification. (Rom. 4:25)

and

> And if Christ has not been raised, your faith is futile, you are still in your sins. Then those also who have fallen asleep in Christ are lost. If only for this life we have hope in Christ, we are to be pitied more than all men. But Christ has indeed been raised from the dead. (1 Cor. 15:17–20)

Because Jesus's love has led the way for us, we should follow him by serving in love, even to the point of giving our lives in his service, looking forward to our promised resurrection. We should always be ready to show the full extent of our love for the Lord God Almighty.

Love Obeys

Because of Christ's death, burial, and resurrection, we have the hope of heaven if we obey God (Heb. 5:8–9). Jesus gave a very important command just before he went back to heaven. If we love him, we will obey every part of this command:

> Then Jesus came to them and said, "All authority in heaven and on earth has been given to me. Therefore go and make disciples of all nations, baptizing them in the name of the Father and of

the Son and of the Holy Spirit, and teaching them to obey everything I have commanded you. And surely I am with you always, to the very end of the age. (Matt. 28:18–20)

If we love him, we will "go," "make disciples," "baptize them," and "teach them to obey everything." If we truly believe what the Lord has told us, we will react in gratitude and thanksgiving. We will gladly obey his will in everything without trying to find a way around it to do what we think is better, and without saying, "Oh, we don't have to obey that. It isn't a salvation issue."

If God wants us to do something, and we do not do it, then it has become a salvation issue. First John 3:10b tells us, "Anyone who does not do what is right is not a child of God" (1 John 3:10b). Later in that same book, we read, "This is love for God: to obey his commands. And his commands are not burdensome" (5:3). Of course, whatever God wants us to do is what is right. We should realize that God's way is always the best way. And we should take him at his word (John 14:15).

We do many things for the Lord, not to earn our salvation (which we could never do), but *because* we have been saved. We want to return the love that God gives us in abundance. As we serve the Lord in love, by his grace we become more like him: "And we ... are being transformed into his likeness with ever-increasing glory, which comes from the Lord, who is the Spirit" (2 Cor. 3:18).

Love Judges

Some people think that there will be universal salvation, that everyone will go to heaven. They think that a loving God would not punish anyone in such a horrible place as hell. However, a just God cannot reward sinfulness. There is no place in heaven for those who do not obey God. Revelation tells us what their place will be:

> He who was seated on the throne said, "I am making everything new!" Then he said, "Write this down, for these words are trustworthy and true."

> He said to me: "It is done. I am the Alpha and the Omega, the Beginning and the End. To him who is thirsty I will give to drink without cost from the spring of the water of life. He who overcomes will inherit all this, and I will be his God and he will be my son. But the cowardly, the unbelieving, the vile, the murderers, the sexually immoral, those who practice magic arts, the idolaters and all liars—their place will be in the fiery lake of burning sulfur. This is the second death." (Rev. 21:5–8)

And 1 Corinthians also tells us,

> Do you not know that the wicked will not inherit the kingdom of God? Do not be deceived: Neither the sexually immoral nor idolaters nor adulterers nor male prostitutes nor homosexual offenders nor thieves nor the greedy nor drunkards nor slanderers nor swindlers will inherit the kingdom of God. And that is what some of you were. But you were washed, you were sanctified, you were justified in the name of the Lord Jesus Christ and by the Spirit of our God. (6:9–11)

What an awesome blessing it is that God loves us so much that he is willing to forgive us when we repent of our sins and turn back to him! No matter how vile our sins have been, God is ready to forgive us and wipe the slate clean, if only we will repent, turn to him, and live our lives in obedience to his will. He wants us to be in heaven with him: "He is patient with you, not wanting anyone to perish, but everyone to come to repentance" (2 Pet. 3:9b).

Love Forgives

As we daily live our lives in love, trying to obey God's will, we gradually become more like God himself. God is holy, and his will is that we also should be holy, that we should be sanctified (1 Thess. 4:3). We are transformed from a life of sin to a life in the light of his presence. Of course, we are still humans, and even though we try to follow God's will, we will still sin. John gives us hope that after sinning we can again become more like God:

> If we claim to be without sin, we deceive ourselves and the truth is not in us. If we confess our sins, he is faithful and just and will

forgive us our sins and purify us from all unrighteousness. (1 John 1:8–9)

and

My dear children, I write this to you so that you will not sin. But if anybody does sin, we have one who speaks to the Father in our defense—Jesus Christ, the Righteous One. He is the atoning sacrifice for our sins, and not only for ours but also for the sins of the whole world. (1 John 2:1–2)

Only Jesus lived a perfect life. But when we sin, we can thank God that it is not the end of the story for us. No matter how bad we are, God forgives and forgets when we repent and ask for forgiveness.

Think of the example of David. God said that David was "A man after my own heart" (Acts 13:22; 1 Sam. 13:14). However, David sinned with Bathsheba, and he caused the death of her husband (2 Sam. 11). How could God possibly say that such a sinful man, an adulterer and a murderer, could be pleasing to him? Because when David was confronted by Nathan and persuaded of his sin, he repented and turned back to God (2 Sam. 12). His heart was broken, and he begged God for forgiveness (2 Sam. 12:13, 16–17, 20).

When we realize our sin, we will be forgiven as David was if we repent and try to follow the Lord again. The number of times that he will forgive us is limited only by the number of times we repent and ask for forgiveness.

However, if we want to be forgiven, we must forgive others (Matt. 6:14–15; Eph. 4:32; Col. 3:13). Peter realized this and asked Jesus, "How many times shall I forgive my brother when he sins against me? Up to seven times?" (Matt. 18:21). Peter may have thought he was being generous, but the answer must have surprised him. The translation of the answer varies. The New International Version says "seventy-seven times"; but the King James Version says: "Seventy times seven." That is four hundred ninety times! Peter surely did not expect that answer, but it emphasizes the unlimited forgiveness that God has for us.

Conclusion

The title of this chapter is "Love Is the Answer." You may have been wondering, what is the question? Actually, love is the answer to many of life's questions. For example, love is the answer to fear. "There is no fear in love. But perfect love drives out fear, because fear has to do with punishment. The one who fears is not made perfect in love" (1 John 4:18). You may be able to think of other questions to which the answer is love. However, the question I have considered is this: What can change my life and help me get to heaven? And love really is the answer.

As we act lovingly, we learn to love. As we learn more, God lavishes his love on us, and we grow in that love. As God's love awakens our love, we imitate his love (Eph. 5:1–2). As his love deepens in us, we show our love by obeying the Lord. As we obey him, we love him more, and as we love him more, we want to study the Bible more to know him better. As we learn more about the Almighty God, the great Creator, we love him more and more. Thus love spirals ever upward until we reach our final destination, where we shall spend eternity basking in the glories of heaven in the presence and love of the Lord.

In the depths of God's wisdom, he has ordained that it takes love to answer the question—both God's love for us and our love for God.

My prayer is that you will come to know the infinite riches of the love of the Lord, and you, like Paul, will spend the rest of your life praising God for his wisdom and love:

> Oh, the depth of the riches of the wisdom and knowledge of God!
> How unsearchable his judgments,
> and his paths beyond tracing out!
> "Who has known the mind of the Lord?
> Or who has been his counselor?"
> "Who has ever given to God,
> that God should repay him?"

For from him and through him and to him are all things.
To him be the glory forever! Amen. (Rom. 11:33–36)

FOR FURTHER THOUGHT

1. How would you explain biblical love to a nonbeliever?

2. How does that love affect your daily life?

3. In what ways has the love of the Lord transformed you?

4. What changes have you made in your lifestyle because of the Lord's love for you? Because of your love for the Lord?

5. What other changes should you make?

6. What does the Lord's resurrection from the dead mean to you?

7. How could someone as sinful as David be pleasing to the Lord? What does that teach you about how you can please the Lord?

8. What is the most important (to you) thing that you have learned from this book?

*Now to him who is able
to do immeasurably more
than all we ask or imagine,
according to his power
that is at work within us,
to him be glory in the church
and in Christ Jesus
throughout all generations,
for ever and ever!
Amen.*
—Ephesians 3:20-21

Endnotes

Chapter One
1. W. Gunther, H.-G. Link, "Love," in Colin Brown, ed., *The New International Dictionary of New Testament Theology*, Vol. 2 (Grand Rapids: Zondervan, 1976), 538, 542.
2. Ibid., 539.
3. Ibid., 539.
4. Ibid., 538.
5. For fuller treatment of this matter, see Nancy Ferguson, "The Agony of the Cross," *Gospel Advocate* 149 (April 2007):13.

Chapter Two
1. Everett Ferguson, *Backgrounds of Early Christianity*, 3rd ed. (Grand Rapids: Eerdmans, 2003), 190–2.
2. Jerome, *Commentary on Galatians* 6.10.

Chapter Three
n/a

Chapter Four
1. C. S. Lewis wrote *The Screwtape Letters*, in which he suggests how Satan works to tempt us to do what he wants. In this book, a senior devil writes to his nephew with advice on how to tempt humans. Lewis has some thought-provoking material in this book that can help us learn to resist Satan's temptations.

Chapter Five
1. For a fuller treatment of the topic of submission, see Nancy Ferguson, "Submission, What's in It for Me?" in *Living a Worthy Life* (Nashville: Gospel Advocate, 1999), pp. 165–192.
2. This verse differs widely in various translations. Other examples include the New Living Translation, which says, "Loyalty makes a person attractive" and the King James Version, which says, "The desire of a man is his kindness."

Chapter Six
1. Helen Steiner Rice wrote a lovely little poem that includes some things done while courting that should continue in marriage. See "What Is Marriage?" in *Poems and Prayers of Helen Steiner Rice* (Grand Rapids: Revell, 2004), 27.
2. J. Allan Petersen, quoted in Louise A. Ferrebee's *The Healthy Marriage Handbook* (Nashville: B&H, 2001), 152

Chapter Seven
1. Taken from *The 30th Anniversary Reader's Digest Reader* (Pleasantville, NY: Reader's Digest Association, 1951), 257.

2. Jess Lair, *"I Ain't Much, Baby—But I'm All I've Got"* (New York: Fawcett, 1995).

Chapter Eight
1. Ann Doyle, used by permission.

Chapter Nine
1. Milton Jones, "A Difficult Verse," *21st Century Christian Magazine* (Jan./Feb. 2005), 28–30.
2. See John 13:34; 15:12,17; Romans 12:10; 13:8; 16:16; 1 Corinthians 16:20; Galatians 5:13,14; Ephesians 4:2; 1 Thessalonians 3:12,4:9-10; 2 Thessalonians 1:3; Hebrews 10:24; 1 Peter 1:22, 5:14; 1 John 3:11,23; 4:7,11,12; and 2 John 5, among others.
3. Jerome, *Commentary on Galatians* 6.10.
4. Often when we read a familiar passage of scripture, the words flow so quickly that our minds wander and we don't pay enough attention to them. It is good to read from a different translation sometimes just to get fresh wording and make us think about what we are reading. I recommend the Contemporary English Version of 1 Corinthians 13, which is printed in the form of a poem.

Chapter Ten
1. Anthony L. Ash wrote a book entitled *Decide to Love, a Biblical Guide to Christian Living* (Austin: Sweet Publishing Company, 1980). In this book, which is unfortunately out of print, he discussed the love that is described in 1 Corinthians 13. I am heavily indebted to Tony and his book for much of the following material, and I thank him for permission to use his book.
2. Frederick William Danker, Walter Bauer, W. F. Arndt, and F. W. Gingrich, *A Greek-English Lexicon of the New Testament and other Early Christian Literature*, 3rd ed. (Chicago: University of Chicago Press, 2000), 427.
3. Ash, 45.
4. Ibid., 64.
5. Danker, et al, 147.
6. Ash, 113–114.
7. Danker, et al, 942.
8. Ibid.
9. Ash, 137.
10. "Tie a Yellow Ribbon 'Round the Old Oak Tree," Irwin Levine and L. Russell Brown, 1972. First recorded as a single by Tony Orlando and Dawn in 1973 on the Bell label; produced by Hank Medress and Dave Appell.

Chapter Eleven
1. See Nancy Ferguson, "The Role of Women in the Assembly of the Church," *Directions for the Road Ahead: Stability in Change Among Churches of Christ*, ed. Jim Sheerer and Charles L. Williams (Chickasha, Oklahoma: Yeomen Press, 1998), 41–53; and Everett Ferguson, *Women in the Church* (Chickasha, Oklahoma: Yeomen Press, 2003).
2. Everett Ferguson, *Church History, Volume One: From Christ to Pre-Reformation* (Grand Rapids: Zondervan, 2005), 156–157.

3. Eusebius, *Church History* 5.1.42, qtd. in Herbert Musurillo, *The Acts of the Christian Martyrs*, Oxford Early Christian Texts (Oxford: Clarendon Press, 1972), 67, 75.
4. Everett Ferguson, *Early Christians Speak*, Vol. 2 (Abilene, Texas: ACU Press, 2002), 274.
5. Ferguson, *Early Christians Speak*, 275
6. Ibid., 275–276.
7. Ibid., 276–277.
8. Ibid., 277.

Chapter Twelve

1. Everett Ferguson, *Backgrounds of Early Christianity*, 3rd ed. (Grand Rapids: Eerdmans, 2003), 127.
2. C. H. Dodd, *The Epistle of Paul to the Romans* (London: Hodder and Stoughton, 1932), 234.
3. Ferguson, 88–90.
4. Ibid., 67.
5. Ibid., 79.
6. L. Michael White, "House Church," *Encyclopedia of Early Christianity*, Vol. 1, eds. Everett Ferguson, Michael P. McHugh, and Fredrick W. Norris, 2nd ed. (New York: Garland [Taylor & Francis], 1997), 546.
7. W. J. Conybeare and J. S. Howson, *The Life and Epistles of St. Paul* (Grand Rapids: Eerdmans Publishing Company, 1951), 534.
8. Frederick William Danker, Walter Bauer, W. F. Arndt, and F. W. Gingrich, *A Greek-English Lexicon of the New Testament and other Early Christian Literature*, 3rd ed. (Chicago: University of Chicago Press, 2000), 230.
9. Henry George Liddell, Robert Scott, and Henry Stuart Jones, *A Greek-English Lexicon*, 9th ed. (Oxford: Clarendon Press, 1953), 398.
10. Charles B. Williams, *The New Testament: A Translation in the Language of the People* (Chicago: Moody Publishers, 1972).
11. Dodd, 234.

Chapter Thirteen

n/a

Scripture Index

For the reader's ease of study, this index provides a comprehensive list of the Scriptural references that appear in this book.

Genesis
1............................34
2:18....................59, 71
2:24....................59, 61
3............................93
17:16......................85
30:6........................85
33:5........................85

Exodus
2:1–10....................91
18:20......................88
20:5......................130
34:14....................130

Leviticus
19:18............115, 136
19:18–19..............116

Numbers
26:59......................91

Deuteronomy
4:24......................130
6:6–9......................87
11:19–20................87
24:1–4....................76
31:12–13................87

Ruth
4:13........................85

1 Samuel
1:26–28................100
2 and 3..................92
13:14....................177
15..........................93
17:38–40................46

2 Samuel
11........................177
12........................177

12:13....................177
12:16–17..............177
12:20....................177

1 Chronicles
1:26–28................100
29:19......................99

Psalm
19:1–4..................172
22:1........................20
22:24......................20
34:11......................87
78:2–7....................88
121:7–8..................34
127:3–4..................85
133:1....................121
136....................17–18
139........................33
139:1–10................43

Proverbs
2:12–19..................67
3:9..........................77
3:33........................61
5:15–23..................67
6:23–29..................67
6:32........................67
11:22......................68
11:28b....................76
12:18......................68
13:10......................73
13:24......................92
14:1........................74
15:1........................73
15:13......................78
15:16–17................60
15:16......................76
16:3........................60
17:1........................73
17:6........................85

17:14......................73
17:22....................105
19:22......................66
21:9........................73
22:6................91, 101
23:4–5....................77
25:24......................73
25:28....................100
27:15–16..........73–74
29:15......................91
29:17......................92
31:10–31................79

Ecclesiastes
12:1........................91

Isaiah
28:10......................91
40:11......................18
41:10......................33
52:7........................51
59:15b–17a............49
66:13......................18

Jeremiah
31:3........................17

Joel
1:3..........................87

Zephaniah
3:17........................18

Malachi
2:16..................63, 76
2:16–17..................68
3:16–18..................18

Matthew
4:1–11....................54
5:16......................123
5:17............119, 126
5:21–22..........119–120

5:44 .... 64, 85, 115	10:38–42 152	2:4 129
6:14–15 .... 142, 177	16:10–12 100	4:8 34
6:33 60	21:1–4 152	4:20–21 173
7:7–8 72	22:25–27 150	4:25 174
7:9–11 .... 24, 72	24:1–11 152	5:1–5 26
7:12 .... 71, 72	**John**	5:7–8 64
8:14–15 152	2:5 .... 152, 167	5:8 19
9:20–22 152	3:16 .... 13, 101, 172	6:1–2 41
12:43–45 37	3:21 123	6:4 34
15:21–28 152	4:28–30 152	8:26–27 112–113
18:21 177	6:28–29 123	8:35 40
18:22 145	6:43 121	8:38–39 .... 20, 24
19:4–6 62	11:27 152	11:33–36 178-179
19:6 .... 63, 76	12:26 167	12:1 117
19:8–9 68	13:1–2 19	12:5 122
19:8b 76	13:1 .... 23, 173	12:9–13 117
19:16–17 123	13:4–5 150	12:10 .... 15, 68, 184
20:20–22 152	13:14–15 122	12:13 123
20:25–28 149	13:34–35 .... 28, 115,	12:14–16 118
20:26 167	126, 184	12:15 123
22:37–38 27	14:15 .... 27, 175	12:16 121
25:31–46 29	14:21 27	12:17–21 118
25:40 .... 124, 162	14:23 27	12:18 74
26:39 30	15:9 102	13:4 167
27:55–56 152	15:12 184	13:8–10 118–119
28:1 152	15:13 19	13:8 184
28:18–20 174–175	15:17 184	13:10 16
Mark	17:11–12 .... 40, 57–58	13:12 146
3:17 .... 31, 119	17:15 .... 40, 57–58	13:14 56
5:25 152	17:20 40	14:19 121
7:24–30 152	20:1–18 152	15:5–6 122
9:50 121	**Acts**	15:7 122
10:16 104	2:42–47 90	15:8 166
11:15–17 138	9:36–43 153	16 .... 153, 159
12:42–44 152	12:12–17 153	16:1–2 .... 159, 165
15:34 20	13:22 177	16:1 159
16:1 152	16:1 153	16:2 163
Luke	16:13–15 153	16:5 163
1:27 152	16:22–25 140	16:13 153
1:30 152	16:40 153	16:16 184
1:38 152	17:11 28	**1 Corinthians**
2:36–37 152	18:2–3 153	1:12 133
6:27–31 123	18:24–26 153	6:9–11 176
6:27 16	**Romans**	6:19–20 25
6:31 86	1:12 121	7:1–7 65
8:1–3 152	1:19–20 172	7:2–5 67
8:43 152	1:31 15	7:5 65
10:25–28 136		7:10 76
		10:13 37

10:24 ... 123
12:25 ... 122
12:31 ... 127
13 ... 124, 125, 127, 137, 144, 146
13:1–3 ... 127
13:2 ... 127
13:4–7 ... 127
13:5 ... 137
13:8–13 ... 127
13:8 ... 143
13:12 ... 146
13:13 ... 145
14:33–37 ... 151
14:33–38 ... 157
14:37 ... 151
15:1–5 ... 174
15:17–20 ... 174
16:14 ... 23, 149
16:15–16 ... 66
16:19 ... 163

2 Corinthians
3:18 ... 175
5:18–21 ... 139
5:21 ... 20, 34, 50
9:8 ... 124
10:13–18 ... 133
11:2–4 ... 131
11:15 ... 167

Galatians
3:27 ... 56
4:17–18 ... 130
5:13–15 ... 30
5:13 ... 122, 149
5:22–26 ... 79
5:22–23 ... 31
6:1 ... 128
6:2 ... 122
6:9–10 ... 124
6:14 ... 133

Ephesians
1:3 ... 35, 133
1:6–8 ... 35
1:18–21 ... 36
1:19–20 ... 34
1:20 ... 41
1:22–23 ... 66
2:1–7 ... 36–37
2:1–2 ... 36
2:4–5 ... 33
2:5 ... 36
2:8–10 ... 122–123, 150
2:8–9 ... 36
2:10 ... 38
2:11–12 ... 37
2:13 ... 37
2:14–18 ... 37
2:19 ... 37, 38
3:6 ... 37
3:10–12 ... 38–39
3:12 ... 37
3:14–21 ... 38
3:16–19 ... 40
3:17–19 ... 21, 23
3:20–21 ... 41, 181
4:2 ... 122
4:15 ... 140
4:10 ... 40
4:17–18 ... 41
4:22–24 ... 41
4:25 ... 77, 122, 141
4:26–27 ... 75
4:27 ... 42
4:32 ... 177
5:1 ... 125
5:1–2 ... 31, 42, 57, 119
5:2 ... 30, 117, 126
5:10–11 ... 42
5:11 ... 43
5:21–6:9 ... 45
5:21–22 ... 65
5:21 ... 66
5:22–33 ... 63, 69–70
5:25 ... 63, 69
5:33 ... 69, 81
6:1–3 ... 88
6:4 ... 86
6:10–18 ... 26, 34–35, 45, 47, 57, 98
6:10 ... 45
6:11 ... 45, 57
6:12 ... 46, 47
6:13 ... 47, 57
6:14 ... 48, 49, 57
6:15 ... 50, 57
6:16 ... 52, 57
6:17 ... 54, 57
6:18 ... 55

Philippians
1:1 ... 167
1:9–11 ... 81
2:3 ... 135
3:8–9 ... 50
3:20 ... 56
4:4–7 ... 31
4:4 ... 59, 140
4:7 ... 51
4:8–9 ... 139
4:13 ... 57

Colossians
1:9–14 ... 43–44
1:21–23 ... 56
1:22 ... 50
2:14 ... 139
3:13 ... 122, 177
3:18 ... 65
3:20 ... 110
4:15 ... 163–164

1 Thessalonians
3:12 ... 78
4:3 ... 176
4:9–10 ... 126
4:18 ... 121
5:8 ... 26
5:11 ... 121
5:17 ... 55
5:22 ... 43

2 Thessalonians
2:10 ... 173

1 Timothy
2:9–15 ... 151
3 ... 67, 79
3:2 ... 168
3:3 ... 15
3:8 ... 167
3:11 ... 168
3:12 ... 168
4:6 ... 167
6:10 ... 76
6:17–18 ... 124

2 Timothy
1:5 ... 88, 153
3:3 ... 15
3:15 ... 88, 153

3:16–17 124
4:18 .... 34, 45

Titus

1 .... 67, 79
1:8 67
2:3–5 151
2:3–4 85
2:4 .... 63, 83
3:1 66
3:3–7 119

Philemon

2 164

Hebrews

4:16 .... 25, 32
5:7–8 66
5:8–9 174
6:10 124
10:24 121
10:25 90
11:1 143
12:2 .... 30, 140
13:1–3 156–157
13:4 .... 59, 67, 81
13:20–21 146

James

2:18–19 173
2:19 48

4:7 66
4:17 124
5:9 121

1 Peter

1:15–16 50
2:9 133
3:15 54
3:21–22 66
5:5–6 66
5:6 135

2 Peter

2:9 34
3:9 .... 129, 176

1 John

1:8–9 176–177
2:1–2 177
2:2 24
2:3–4 28
2:3–6 173
3:1 .... 24, 119, 133
3:10 .... 119, 175
3:12 119
3:15 120
3:16–20 120
3:16 .... 13, 23
3:17–18 29
3:18 .... 64, 120

4:1 142
4:7–12 120
4:7 .... 28, 171
4:8 .... 13, 14, 32, 125
4:9–11 119
4:9 19
4:10–11 17
4:11 .... 111, 115
4:16–21 120
4:16 .... 13, 14, 19, 125
4:18 178
4:19–21 19
4:19 .... 29, 119
4:20–21 ...... 29, 117, 143
4:21 120
5:1–3 120
5:3 .... 14, 27, 175
5:13 173

Jude

21 61
24–25 169–170

Revelation

1:16 54
2:10 144
12:9–10 34
21:5–8 175–176
21:27 .... 139, 152

About the Author

Nancy Ferguson graduated from Abilene Christian College in 1955 with a B.A. in Bible. She has written Vacation Bible School materials and articles for *Power for Today*, *Gospel Advocate*, *21st Century Christian*, and *Church and Family*. Her chapter "The Role of Women in the Assembly of the Church" appeared in *Directions for the Road Ahead: Stability in Change among Churches of Christ*, and her previous book, *Living a Worthy Life* (Gospel Advocate, 1999), has been translated into Russian. Nancy has taught classes at lectureships, ladies' days, workshops, retreats, and more in at least six U.S. states and eight foreign countries. Her topics have included teacher training, family relationships, women's roles in the church, submission, and various passages from Scripture. She currently teaches ladies' Bible classes, and is active in ministries to mothers of young children and to international students at Abilene Christian University. Nancy married Everett Ferguson in 1956. They have three children and six grandchildren.

www.ingramcontent.com/pod-product-compliance
Lightning Source LLC
Chambersburg PA
CBHW020651300426
44112CB00007B/329